CONFUSED
ABOUT CARE FOR YOUR
MUM AND DAD?

The Guidebook on all the Best Solutions

FOREWORD BY
MARK DENTON BEVENS
Author of What is Graves Disease: Surviving Hyperthyroidism

AVRIL TABUNS

BONUSES
INCLUDES HOW TO PREPARE A LEGAL DIY WILL.
Home Care checklist, Nursing Home checklist,
Tools to assess for dementia and mobility and other health risks
PLUS A Legal Guide for Older People Comprehensive E Book and lots more!!!

ISBN: 978-1-4834-2502-3 (sc)
ISBN: 978-1-4834-2501-6 (e)

Library of Congress Control Number: 2015901270

Because of the dynamic nature of the Internet, any web addresses or
links contained in this book may have changed since publication and
may no longer be valid. The views expressed in this work are solely those
of the author and do not necessarily reflect the views of the publisher,
and the publisher hereby disclaims any responsibility for them.

Any people depicted in stock imagery provided by Thinkstock are models,
and such images are being used for illustrative purposes only.
Certain stock imagery © Thinkstock.

Lulu Publishing Services rev. date: 04/13/2015

DEDICATION

This book is lovingly dedicated to my dad Garry Semple.

He visited me in spirit through a medium. She
told me he was holding a book, a book I would
write within the next year or so.....

At that time I had no thoughts about
writing this book or any other.

Thank you dad for always believing in me and loving me.

Contents

Preface

I decided to write this book for two reasons, one because of my of experience working with families through Casa A Carers, who provide a live in home care service for two specific groups the elderly and infirm, and individuals with mental or physical disabilities. Two because I got into the care business as my own mother, made it very clear she would rather die than go into a nursing home, and neither would I.

Having an elderly mother and being the wrong side of fifty, I also started thinking about what kind of care I would like when my time came.

In the past few years we have watched shocking documentaries of abuse in nursing homes, and observed care staff who were rough, inconsiderate bullies.

This has compelled me to create a model of service, which is affordable and practical and allows everyone the right to choose to remain at home.

I lived in Asia for many years, and would have been largely unavailable to help my parents. This is common now among families as some siblings may live overseas and some may live far from the family home.

This means that the adult child or children living within commuting distance have to share the caring duties when their Mum or Dad need some extra help or have a period of Illness.

As I write this I am in Scotland as recently, my mother has been extremely ill.

This past year I have had to drop everything to be with my Mum on and off as she was really poorly for over a month before being hospitalized for 7 weeks. There were times during this period I had to face the facts that I may lose her as the doctors could not find the source of her suspected infection.

Also during this time a client of mine was hospitalized with the same symptoms but sadly she did not survive.

I am just like you, going through all the issues covered in this book.

I also am a mother and have 3 children, so I am very aware of what my clients are going through and the resentment among siblings and the resentment of our Mums or Dad's thinking we're "meddling" in their affairs.

Very often I get a call in desperation as my clients Mum or Dad has had an episode in hospital, and has increasing care needs, the social work team have suggested 24/7 care and have given a list of nursing homes.

The people who call me know their Mum or Dad will be most unhappy in a nursing home, yet they can't provide the care required, are worried about costs and also there seems to be so many different agencies and so many different prices, there are schemes in Ireland like the Home Care Package, Home Help, and a scheme where you commit the sale of your house to the government to cover your care cost called "The Fair Deal" Scheme.

They have to get care sorted usually within a matter of days, as their Mum or Dad is being discharged and this is a mine field for them, they feel pressured and also there may be a number of siblings involved in making the decision as they may also need to sort out how they will pay, who will pay and how much.

Everyone has a different opinion and no one can agree, usually one person is left to make all the enquiries, but unable to make the decision alone.

Then your Mum or Dad is resistant to the idea of having a "Stranger" in their home and their loss of advocacy, and they feel sure they will be able to manage if only their children all lend a hand.

I have experienced this first hand and I know from working with families how stressful this is and no one really knows for sure the outcomes.

Are they making the best decision?

Have they considered all the options?

What about longer term, will this solution be viable in the long term what if Mum or Dad deteriorates?

What if Mum or Dad don't like the person assigned to their care?

What if we don't like the carer?

I wrote this book because it would be much easier if you could have all the information to hand, and have resources (financial, legal, health and safety) to help you make these decisions.

I would really love it to be a helpful handbook to help families of parents who are obviously at a certain age or stage of decline to start the discussion before an accident happens.

My initial reason for writing the book was as a resource for Irish families as this is where I operate my home care businesses, however as I wrote the book I realized there is a much bigger market needing this information so instead of re writing the whole book and including information for lots of other countries. I decided to create multiple supplementary resource guides country by country which are in a PDF format easily downloadable from the book website together with the published bonuses www.care-for-mum-and-dad.com

Then choices can be made in advance, plans can be written down with different steps for different stages and the solutions for each of these stages. A cohesive plan that everyone is agreed upon.

The children of elderly parents will usually be in their late forties to sixties and will also benefit from exploring all these options and start thinking about their own old age, and what they would like to happen when it's their turn.

Somehow when it seems a bit far away it is easier to consider what you want for yourself, as there is some detachment involved.

Getting older is a fact, and planning makes everything much better and saves lots of sleepless night and stress for everyone.

I hope you find all the answers to the questions you may have, and this becomes a good family activity, and brings families closer together, maybe your teenagers can also become involved so it becomes a TRI -Generational planning activity.

I have included quite a few FREE extra bonus resources available on my website.

www.care-for-mum-and-dad.com

I hope the information and resources are both helpful and informative to allow you and your loved ones to make the right decision for your family.

I am happy to have feedback and answer any questions go to the contact us section on my website.

Lastly, keep it light hearted and bring your sense of humour along to make this activity more enjoyable and stress free for everyone.

To your success
Avril Tabuns

Foreword

When Avril first approached me about writing a forward for this long anticipated book, I was both honoured and perplexed in equal measure! I was of course honoured because of Avril's international credentials both personally and professionally. Besides running her two successful business's, Home Help Recruitment and Casa A Carers, Avril is also an accomplished life and business coach, certified as a trainer of Hypnosis & NLP, and because I know you will learn more about Avril's many accomplishments later on in this book, I want to move swiftly on to the perplexed part!

Why would the wonderful Avril Tabuns ask me to write a forward for a book called 'Confused About Care For Your Mum And Dad: *The guide book on all the best solutions.*'

What did I know about care facilities and solutions! Absolutely NOTHING, and that my friend is the whole point of this remarkable book, written by someone not only on the inside of the care business as an informed provider, but also by someone with their own worries and concerns about an elderly parent.

For many, myself included, talk of care facilities with a parent is a taboo subject. And that taboo is predominantly brought about by ignorance of the facts, an ignorance born by burying our head in the sand. *'Of course it won't happen to anyone in our family. That stuff happens to others...'* And so we walk around ignoring the fact that we may not always be able to care for our elderly loved ones, because of course we are always going to be young fit and financially able to take care of them ourselves! But the sad reality is, that's not always the reality, and life can sometimes deal you some uncomfortable blows.

As a Breakthrough Coach, I have come to understand that many of life's challenges are brought about by a lack of preparation, and that is ultimately what this book is all about. Knowledge is power. It gives you the ability to control the situation rather than the situation controlling you. So until or unless you are clear about what type of care would be best for your Mum and Dad, or how you will deal with all the legal aspects that may come your way, and more importantly how you are going to fund all of this care, you had better read this heart felt, information packed gem of a book from cover to cover, because like it or not, your parent's future comfort and security may just depend on it.

Thank you Avril for taking the time to compile and create this much needed resource.

Love & Light
Mark Denton Bevens

www.MarkDentonBevens.com Image Mark Bevens

Acknowlegements

I would like to especially thank Mark Denton Bevens, Bernadette Parte and Mary Rafferty, for sharing their expertise and their valuable contributions to this book and bonuses.

A big thank you to Harriet Pritchard for her excellent research in all aspects and service available for care internationally

Firstly, I would like to thank my parents Trina and Garry Semple without you I wouldn't exist or be who I am today, without your loving guidance and continuous support, and personal sacrifices throughout my life.

I would like to share a deeply personal moment and thank my dad for having the courage on his deathbed to share his regrets and short -comings as a father.

"Grow old along with me! The best is yet to be." Robert Browning (1812-1889)

It has left a deep and lasting impression on me to try not to be in that same position (*dying with regrets of lost opportunities and not doing the important things I should have*).

He taught me to live each day to the best of my abilities, to try to achieve all my goals and remember what is truly important – love, gratitude and family.

My mother taught me unconditional love, and that life is too short for holding grudges or anger. She also taught me never to judge "as there for the Grace of God go I" she was a nurse and devoted much of her life to the care of others.

She is now in her eighties and needs our care, but up to a year or so ago tried to do more than she should for her grandchildren.

I would also like to thank my grandmothers, both strong women who lived through 2 wars, who taught me perseverance, love of God and the saints-(that was my Irish Granny I loved praying the Rosary with her and chatting about what Heaven would be like.)

My teachers and coaches past and present David Shepard, Dr Garry Yardley, Dr Joanna Martin, Paul Davis, Arnold La Spina, Gil Boyne, Brian Tracey, Raymond Aaron, Anthony Robbins and Marion Boon.

All my clients for sharing their lives and stories with me and letting me have the honour to care for their loved ones. My Clients who have passed and with whom I still pray for, talk to, ask for help and remember with much love.

My children for understanding that sometimes I was too busy to give them all the time they wanted and for being proud of me despite my short comings.

My ex husband Roy Bhasker and wonderful father of our 3 children.

My husband and best friend and business partner Maris Tabuns for tolerating me, supporting me, loving me unconditionally and always believing in me.

I would also like to acknowledge you, for getting this book and having the desire to do the very best for your loved ones, and allowing me to share a little of myself. Thank You

CHAPTER 1
Signs of Change

Life is ever moving ever changing and as my father often said

"There is only one thing in life you can be certain of, and that is, someday you will die."

I remember thinking when I was much younger," What a morbid thing to say," now life is catching up on me, I too am aware of my own mortality.

My Father has long since passed, and my mother now in her 80's is starting to get frail.

Most of us just take for granted our Mum's and Dad's will always be there to help us and comfort us, we tend not to notice the signs until they are too obvious for us to miss.

If you have teenagers, you will understand this, they are so wrapped up in themselves they wouldn't even notice if you grew another head or lost a limb.

"The afternoon knows what the morning never suspected."
— *Robert Frost*

I guess we are all guilty of this, as we are all busy with our lives and the multiple roles we must fill each and every day;- mother/father, daughter/son, sister/brother, wife/husband, friend, employee or boss.

Stress of change

Finding yourself in the position of having to attend to the needs of your Mum and Dad and help them come to terms with the need for change. Whilst often-battling with your siblings who may have opposing ideas, which can be stressful for all concerned.

This is a very confusing and exhausting time for most families.

For many the frustration lies in the fact that there doesn't seem to be an abundance of good information freely available or a step-by-step guide to follow.

Many families are very confused about which type of care would be best for their Mum and Dad.

- ➢ They are also concerned about all the legal considerations that can be involved:- Like do they have a will?
- ➢ What if they become mentally incapacitated?
- ➢ Who will be able to make decisions for them when they are no longer able to administer their own affairs?
- ➢ How will their care be funded?
- ➢ Are there grants available?

> ➢ What about their property can it be used as a source of funding?

The questions go on and on and you also have to remember your Mum and Dad will be highly resistant to change, and giving up control of their affairs.

Spotting the Signs

I have a vast experience with Dementia and old age and unless your Mum or Dad has always been a complainer, it is difficult to really notice these changes in a timely manner.

Sometimes they can be perfect one day then the next day they suffer from an acute and un-expected illness and will never be the same again, and this can happen almost overnight, without any warning signs.

People as they age become aware of their short -comings and ever growing memory loss and forgetfulness, and like we do, they adapt with coping strategies.

Very often people can cover up very convincingly and it is not until an accident happens that we become fully aware of the gravity of the situation.

This is when the care team in a hospital will do an assessment called CSAR★, (copy available at www.care-for-mum-and-dad. com) and will often suggest a nursing home should be considered as the best route.

Note★ I have covered a little later the latest information on schemes and there are charities in Ireland like Age Action, Alone, Older and Bolder challenging the government to bring in better policies and grants to enable more people to remain at home with assistance. I have included information for other countries in the Bonuses on my website.

Here are some of the tell tale signs that all is not as it appears to be:

- *Their driving is not safe anymore.*
- *Unpaid bills are lying around.*
- *The phone, electricity or gas gets cut off.*
- *There is very little food in the fridge, or moldy food and jars not thrown out.*
- *They will have packets of biscuits and cakes, but not much else in the cupboards.*
- *They are wearing the same clothes and they are a bit disheveled.*
- *The house is unkempt and clutter is gathering.*
- *The kitchen and bathroom are not very clean.*
- *They miss appointments.*
- *They have been losing weight*
- *There seems lots of medication lying around and some is out of date.*
- *They are not reading their newspapers; they seem depressed, listless and disinterested.*
- *Mum used to love her daily trip to the local shop but now can't be bothered.*

Some of this may seem extreme, however many families live far apart and may chat on the phone and assume all is well until they visit or a neighbour or friend calls with some concerns.

I had a client once who had to organize care for an unmarried aunt, apparently she had become forgetful and incontinent, she just took the soiled bed linen and underwear off and hid them in drawers and in the wardrobe.

She lived alone and it was only after she had, had a fall, which required a hospital stay, did anyone realise there was a problem.

We also had another client who was quite a celebrity in his day in Ireland and he had dementia and paranoia, however when I visited him he had perfected the perfect cover up (remember preforming was his life) he could talk perfectly, constructing coherent sentences, he even gave me a copy of his book, and signed it. He told me in great detail about his showbiz life and family.

One would never have guessed he had quite bad dementia, as he regularly called the police at night and said he was being kidnapped and couldn't get out of his house.

Accepting reality

So now you realize it is time… Your Mum or Dad needs help.

Now your mind kicks into overdrive, are you and you alone going to be responsible for your parents care?

Will your siblings be able to help or contribute?
Where do you start?
How do you initiate the conversation about your concerns?
What about finances?
Do they have insurance policies?
How much money do they have in the bank?
Do they have any investments?
Have they made a will?
Who will pay for ongoing care?
Do they have Medical Insurance?
What if they need extensive and repeated surgery or medical treatments, does their medical insurance cover this?
Do they have enough money to pay for long-term care?
Do they need medical assessments by specialists?
What about plans if they pass over, have they a written directive?
Do they own a burial plot?
Have they paid into any fund for funeral expenses?
The questions go on and on……..

Trust me in hindsight our family should have had this conversation when we were all at home together for my mother's 70th Birthday. My father passed suddenly 10 weeks later, and he left no will, he assumed it was automatic his widow inherits all.

She is now under duress as she has had to engage a solicitor to sort out his estate and has unpaid taxes due going back over13 years.

She is now in her mid 80's and when I was home taking care of her, being the eldest I brought up the subject of her making a will and sorting out her affairs. She told me she doesn't want to think about it, and she is still sorting out my fathers' affairs.

She said how could she even think about that until my father's affairs are settled. She accused me of being morbid as she is not ready to die yet, and all this talk of wills is stressing her out.

She did come round a few days later and said maybe we should draw up some sort of a will, as she wanted to leave various little keepsakes for her grandchildren. We also suggested sorting out power of attorney to help alleviate any worries should she become very ill or incapacitated, finally she agreed and a will was drawn up, plus she gave power of attorney to my brother and I.

This was very timely as just after this she became very ill and was in hospital for seven weeks. Having everything sorted was one less worry. We were not sure at times if she would survive this illness. (The doctors have still not discovered where the infection site was) She did not improve and was still poorly after 6 weeks of antibiotics. Finally the doctors tried steroids to treat inflammation as no infection was found and thankfully she started to improve, however she has deteriorated so much and recently, has had lots of falls. Sadly she is also extremely confused and her short- term memory has declined significantly,

I have been dealing with families for over 13 years now and really understand how difficult this is as we can be super successful in our

lives and careers but when it comes to family matters you have to deal with multiple ego's, emotions and lots of old unresolved hurts. In most families there are elements of sibling rivalry, which have been established since childhood.

Irrespective of the fact you could often be running multiple companies and have super successful careers, but when you get back home you can often turn back time and become like squabbling children all over again. You are all still able to wind each other up and push all the right buttons, which can cause you to lose your cool and become a screaming wreck, or reticent and moody.

I am sure you get the picture?

I have met only a few families who can put all this aside and have parents who seem to be sensible and willing to have a rational conversation about what they desire for the future and are willing to reveal all their private information to their children.

These are the exceptions rather than the majority.

The majority of families feel they are dysfunctional, as there are unresolved issues, some not talking to others, jealousy and so on. Trust me this is normal not dysfunctional.

Facts to consider about the current situation in Ireland*

Population growth in Ireland far exceeds the EU norms and the only exception is Malta.

The population in 2014 is heading for 6.5 million Ireland has not seen such a large population boom since 1851, however then the population would have had a much higher percentage of young people and children.

Nowadays the number of over 65's represents about 11.5% of the population and projected figures are by 2025 it will be about 25% or 1in 4 people will be over 65.

This seems to be a Global trend and a Global problem and as we live longer and have fewer children, there will be a disproportionate number of older people to young people, who will be able to support the ageing population.

Since 1995 The Irish Government have implemented tax incentives to increase the number of beds from 10,500 by operators in private nursing homes, this could have led to some operators getting into the nursing home business predominately for profit only rather than a desire to work with the elderly and infirm, and create high quality homes.

This could have in some cases led to bad management and cost cutting with low staff to patient ratios, as profit is the main aim of these operators.

More than 17,000 beds have become available since 1995 and now there are currently about 21,500 beds and only 6,500 in the private sector.

In 2010 the government closed 758 public beds and in 2011 there are plans to close another 890 beds.

Costs are cited as the main reason as in the private sector nursing homes average €900+ per week per bed and the public sector the average is about €1,300+

From my research it appears there are may problems in the HSE budgets, and projections for funding and costs and in 2010 the "Fair Deal had to be suspended due to lack of funds, in November 2011 the health minister has had a massive over run in his budget and is looking for a huge amount to cover the costs, this usually comes from the tax payers (you and I)

From what I can gather the public sector has older buildings and more money would be required to renovate and maintain so the government find it more cost effective to close them down and sub contract to the private sector and of course they are shopping for a bargain, and want the lowest priced beds they can avail of.

The fair deal is currently under review and for this I am truly grateful as it is not in fact a "FAIR DEAL ", at all as it applies only to people taking up nursing home beds, and not getting a "Fair Deal" to stay at home.

The following is an excerpt from Alone's website an Irish Charity who work to assist older people who are alone and need assistance

Review of the Fair Deal Scheme

ALONE has welcomed the announcement by Minister of State for Older People Kathleen Lynch TD that she intends to review the Fair Deal Nursing Home Scheme.

We welcome the opportunity to review a system that has a lot of good thinking in it but falls down in terms of implementation; a lack of training for people who are doing the assessments and long waiting lists. (In our experience, for their figures, the HSE calculates the end of the process at assessment whereas the application process has only begun at that stage and can continue for months...)

When the scheme was introduced we welcomed the shift in focus to equal consideration of care in the person's home, with more acute residential care where absolutely necessary. Home care is still considerably cheaper than the long-term residential option and is the preferred option for nearly everybody.

Unfortunately, in our experience, where the Care Needs Assessment is used at all, it is being used just to decide whether somebody should be placed in long-term care or not. (Many HSE assessors still use the Common Summary Assessment Report CSAR* form which was much more focused on the residential care option.) Where it is decided that a person's care needs might be better managed with a Home Care Support Package this support is not available. (for more information on Alone visit www.alone.ie)

CSAR form available www.care-for-mum-and-dad.com

I totally agree as generally this has been my experience completely over the past decade or more, as very often we are called when a fall has occurred or an acute illness requires someone to be hospitalized, when this happens the patient is assessed and if they need quite a bit of help, then nursing homes are always advised, as the first and best option.

Despite the fact that most people want to remain at home, and families are conflicted and confused. In Ireland the doctor is revered second only to the Catholic priest as an authority who should be obeyed.

A Sad Tale

A few years ago I was called to supply urgent care to an elderly lady, however as she deteriorated so fast she was hospitalized within the hour.

2 days later I visited her and asked her would she like to go home and have live in care, her face lit up and she was delighted.

Medically she was fine she had just become severely dehydrated, as we had had several hot days that week (Unusual, I know for Ireland).

Anyone who stops learning is old, whether at 20 or 80. Anyone who keeps learning stays young. The greatest thing in life is to keep your mind young.
— Henry Ford Quotes

When she was admitted she was confused and very weak, yet within hours of receiving fluids intravenously she was back to normal.

This lady was the sweetest person I have ever met.

When I was out visiting her a couple of weeks later, when she had fully recovered due to round the clock care by us, she was talking about how bad she had become and how ill she had been, and couldn't believe how well she felt now she had her 2 special devoted carers.

She had, had an episode a few months previously where she had become depressed and had started to neglect herself.

She had lost lots of weight and wasn't cooking or eating properly.

A social worker was called in and she was assessed by a healthcare team, she was then declared incompetent, which meant there was a process initiated, and her case was assigned to a solicitor, which would then allow the state to make her a ward of court. (*This meant she had no access to her money or had power of attorney over her own affairs, in effect she lost her right to make decisions for herself*)

This lady was neither delusional nor incompetent, she was lucid and rational, she had no family, her husband had passed years earlier and had left her very comfortable.

I asked could she be reassessed and was told it was too late as the process had started.

Out of the blue a month or so later, she just passed in her carers arms, we were all so sad, she was a living angel.

I share this story not to make myself look good by taking her on without even knowing if we would get paid.

My point is to illustrate that due to an illness she was not 100%, and had then been declared incompetent and couldn't get this reversed, she had no sons or daughters to protect her or fight her corner.

This lady was in her 80's and was very competent and lucid.

My most recent experience of this was when my own mother was hospitalized and very unhappy and wanted to come home as the doctors could not find out the source of inflammation or infection causing her to have temperature spikes as soon as the antibiotics were stopped.

The doctor informed me my mother was in not in a position mentally to make decisions, as she had become very confused. Therefore the doctors would prohibit her, the right to discharge herself, or allow us from taking her home. I was infuriated and told the doctor, I thought this was illegal to detain someone against their wishes?

The doctor said they could do this and it has been done before!!

She then said my mum told her she was having a baby! Now when I asked my mum about this she said she had terrible nightmares at night in the hospital and dreamt she had 10 children. My guess was the doctor spoke to her while she was in a dream state. So her eyes were open but she was talking rubbish.

Had my mother not have had any family she could have very easily been declared incompetent and legally made a ward of the court and all her freedom of choice would have been removed.

"You don't stop laughing when you grow old, you grow old when you stop laughing."
— George Bernard Shaw

I find this really frightening and for all the older people whose families are not prepared to question or fight for the rights of their elderly loved ones, as in Ireland you never question the priest or the doctor, as they are (were) held in a sub class of Demi Gods.

I urge you to take this on board even for yourself and get your affairs in order, have clear documents outlining your wishes should you become incompetent.

Have a couple of power of attorneys, you trust to follow your wishes.

I have a special chapter on this by a solicitor who is solely dedicated to people over 50.

I am passionate because someday this will be you and I and if we don't prepare ourselves legally plus demand better services and innovative planning for the future we will be at breaking point, as the numbers of older persons to working adults paying taxes will be out of balance and we or the governments of the future will be unable to finance better services.

Perhaps they will send us all out to space to retirement colonies, joking aside this will be a huge global issue.

What are your concerns?

I have tried to cover all the questions we are concerned about most.

I have also included Bonus materials which can be downloaded and printed from our website <u>www.care-for-mum-and-dad.com</u> ★ here you will find information for many countries including The UK, Australia and New Zealand and I hope to include resources for USA and some European countries too.

These extra products will assist you in getting started and help you create a blueprint of all the important issues that need to be raised in your family discussions.

What is covered?

Firstly a general overview of all services currently available, in Ireland★, links to all the resources for all the services available, and how to get access to funds.

I have given an overview of the pros and cons of each based on my opinion and those of my clients.

I have tried to answer all the questions, which I know myself and other families will face.

Questions such as:

Will we take care of our parents ourselves?

How will we do this?

Which family member is most suited or has fewer responsibilities?

Which family member has the space if Mum or Dad were to move in?

Is it viable to build a purpose built" Granny Flat"?

What will this cost the main carer in regards to loss of privacy, loss of income or opportunities, loss of freedom, pressure on his or her spouse and children and their family dynamics?

How long will this be viable for and when would it be time to consider alternatives?

How can we, or our parents pay for care in the long term?

What funding and help is available?

Do they have a suitable property for modification to accommodate mobility issues such as a stair lift, grab bars in a purpose built bathroom/wet room?

What about security systems?

Do we/they have the financial resources to fund these renovations?

What grants are available to assist them?

Which one of us in the family will assume responsibility for our parents, finances, day-to-day needs?

Have they written a will, do they know where all their policy documents, house deeds are?

How can we share the responsibility of care in an equitable way?

How can we talk about this to our parents?

When is the best time to start planning?

Where do we start?

How do we get started?

In this book I have tried to cover all the main information you will need to know, so you are armed with everything you need and hopefully manage to sort out all your parents care needs and are already thinking about your own future.

I have tried to cover as much information as possible and included specific aforementioned Bonus materials available from the website to download

CHAPTER 2
The Good Old Days

Change is part and parcel of the life and times of humanity, and of course things are different now compared to even 100 years ago.

Life expectancy has gone up significantly, we are living longer than at any time in the documented past, and the forecast for dementia based on current figures is one in five will be afflicted by 2025.

The aging population is growing, and because we choose to have smaller families the burden of caring for our elders falls on a small number of siblings.

Demographically we are more spread out than we were in the past. A hundred years ago it was common to be born and to die in the same village or town, and very often your married children also lived close by.

Families often worked in the same jobs. Traditionally sons followed in their fathers' footsteps and started their employment either in a small family or local business or in local industry or agriculture.

Mums stayed at home so life was different back then and caring for elderly parents was simpler.

Very often as the children moved out an elderly parent may move in especially if their spouse had passed away. Very often families lived within walking distance of each other, so doing errands, cooking and checking in on Mum or Dad was easier.

"How many loved your moments of glad grace, And loved your beauty with love false or true; But one man loved the pilgrim soul in you, And loved the sorrows of your changing face."
— *W.B. Yeats, The Collected Poems*

Both my grandmothers were brought to live beside us in accommodation provided by my Mum and Dad. This was quite popular about 30 -50 years ago people built on a granny flat to their homes.

In this respect I was very blessed as I had both Grandmothers living very close by and both were very different, which meant, I could escape from my family and get some personal one on one time, being the eldest this was great for me.

I remember falling out with my Mum and declared I was leaving home when I was about 8. So I packed a bag and went to stay with my Nana, (Mum's Mum) who lived 2 doors away.

My brother and his family stay next door to my Mum and my nephew has also pulled this stunt and moved in with his Nana (My Mum) for a while.

When I was a young child I loved listening to all the stories my grandmothers told me about the good old days. I also enjoyed catching any gossip, I wasn't supposed to hear as it made me feel so grown up and important.

I vividly remember repeating one such piece of overheard gossip, which caused my parents to squirm red faced and gob smacked. I soon learned what the saying "Walls have ears" meant, and also never to open my big mouth again.

It's not that families love their parents any less it is just the times we live in make this type of intergenerational closeness difficult.

As I mentioned earlier, I lived many years in Asia and there families have a great sense of respect and duty for their elders and also they do not have the social welfare systems that we have in Ireland, UK Europe and the USA.

Therefore many families would have an extended tri-generational household and married children would depend on their parents for childcare and then in return have to care for their parents when they became less capable.

They also had the advantage of employing reasonably costing domestic help from their poorer neighbours such as Philippines and Indonesia.

When I first came back to Ireland from Malaysia, I had 3 young children and the mothers I met were all complaining about the prohibitive cost of childcare and the limited number of places available.

I had just come from a culture where most people had live in help at home.

So that was when I decided to set up my first home based business to help families in Ireland solve their childcare, housekeeping and care needs.

I had no idea how to go about setting up a business in Ireland or that to set up a recruitment business required Garda vetting and a lengthy process to obtain a recruitment license which is required in Ireland.

I called a trusted friend in Malaysia and she recruited and vetted very experienced nannies and carers that wanted to come to Ireland, and I found them families here in Ireland.

I did my research and complied with all the legislation and soon was ready to welcome my first carer from Malaysia

When I started at first I had no money and could not afford to advertise or print brochures.

So if we went away for a weekend perhaps to Galway, or Waterford I put up a small notice in a few supermarkets, advertising my services.

I soon started to get calls; I then got information from my clients on where I could advertise cheaply.

From this grew a reputable solid business and I built a reputation of supplying really good staff all over Ireland.

My business grew mainly through word of mouth and I became the go to person to get really good Filipino staff from Malaysia and the Philippines.

My client list became like a who's, who directory.

Many of my nannies and carers stayed for years with the families and many now are Irish citizens and have settled here permanently.

In 2007 my husband and I founded Casa A Carers. My children were now growing up and all in school so as a natural progression I started to gravitate more towards caring for the elderly. Especially, as my mother was getting on in years and made it clear she would rather die than ever be put in a nursing home.

So here I am writing this book to help you navigate your way through all the options and hopefully get you motivated to get involved in demanding better choices for our generation for when our time comes to require help in the activities of daily living (ADL)

> *And in the end, it's not the years in your life*
> *that count. It's the life in your years.*
> — *Abraham Lincoln Quotes*

Life Today

Today our lives are changing and to maintain a decent lifestyle usually both parents must work.

In addition to work, we often have many other jobs like cooking, shopping, housework and kids that need to be driven everywhere.

For success at work you also need to network and socialize to rise in the job.

So time, is a valuable commodity and we all don't seem to have enough of it nowadays!

Also families move away from the family home and birthplace and travel to get a job or be where their spouse has a job, so commuting for families can be several hours to visit their Mum or Dad and sometimes one or two siblings actually live overseas.

This means the burden of care can usually fall on the shoulders of one child (usually a daughter)

This causes problems too as siblings feel, not everyone cares in the same measure or is willing to help out equally.

This is where we are generally starting from, families separated by distance and feelings of unfairness between them.

I am a therapist and if you want to see mature adults revert in moments to squabbling children with all their family baggage, then put them in a room to sort out how they will share the care for their parents.

Many tell me "our family is dysfunctional you must excuse us," however this is fairly normal for most families, mine included.

Nowadays, we do have some options and this book is about giving you plenty of valuable information and resources to enable you and your family to remain civilized and mature and come to a great decision that your Mum and Dad and the whole family are happy with.

As I mentioned before I realize in hindsight this planning and family conversation should have taken place when I was in my 40's and my parents were both in their 70's and still reasonably fit.

It is definitely much harder as they get older as they just don't want to get stressed thinking about it.

Many families have siblings who don't talk and don't want to get involved and this adds to the stress of the ones who are left to sort things out.

I have included a chapter by a very talented lady who is a communications and mediation expert. I hope this will assist families to heal old wounds and to put aside, old past hurts and issues and begin to function with love and as a whole again.

I will reiterate again I have included many FREE Bonuses available from the website to assist you in all aspects of creating the right plans for your Mum and Dad and you.

I will also cover, adjusting your plans as one parent passes away or their mobility or health becomes further compromised.

In Ireland there is not the amount of choices that are currently available in The UK or USA. *www.care- for- mum- and- dad.com Download your FREE Bonus "International Comprehensive care guide"*

Lets explore what is available for the over 65's today.

Community Care

Health Service Executive H.S.E.

Their responsibility is to deliver, public health, community and home care in Ireland.

They provide the following services in the community:-

1. Public Health Nurses
2. Home Care Attendants
3. Home Helps
4. Physiotherapists
5. Occupational therapists

Public Health Nurses

Public health nurses in Ireland are employed by the HSE to provide a range of health care services in the community.

They are usually based in your local health centre and are assigned to cover specific geographical areas.

They provide services in schools, health centres, day-care and other community centres and in people's homes.

Public health nursing teams provide basic nursing care, as well as advice and assistance to their patients.

They provide planned essential weekend nursing.

Public health nurses also act as an important point of access for other community care services.

Home Helps

Home helps may be employed directly by the HSE or by voluntary organizations on behalf of the HSE.

They assist with normal household tasks such as shopping and cleaning and are assigned to people who are unable to carry out such tasks themselves. Availability varies greatly from place to place. There may be a small charge, even for medical card holders.

Occupational Therapists and Physiotherapists

The HSE employs Occupational and Physiotherapists to help people with disabilities and older people to achieve maximum independence in the activities involved in daily living.

The may be assigned after an operation to help with recovery at home.

Priority is usually given to older people and people with disabilities, as there is a significant shortage of qualified personnel.

Home Care Attendant

Home care attendants provide assistance and support to people with physical disabilities in their own homes.

The time the attendant spends in each person's home and the tasks carried out vary from person to person.

They will help get patients up in the morning, go to the toilet, and get ready for bed.

Dependent on your area it may be a home care attendant who gives a shower or the community nurse

Meals on Wheels

A meals-on-wheels service is quite widely available. It is usually provided by voluntary organizations, who will deliver a balanced meal to people who would find cooking, shopping difficult.

Sign Language Interpreters

Sign language interpretation is used in various situations to facilitate communication between deaf and hearing people. These include medical appointments, job interviews, meetings, conferences and education.

Apply to: Sign Language Interpreting Service (SLIS), c/o Citizens Information Board, Hainault House, The Square, Tallaght, Dublin 24

Social Workers

The HSE employs social workers that can provide advice and support. Most large hospitals employ social workers with whom patients and their relatives can discuss problems arising from their illness.

Ask at the social work department of the hospital. Some voluntary organisations also employ social workers.

Contact: your Local Health Office or public health nurse for more information www.socialwork.ie

Has a list of over 100 day care centers nationwide and you need to be referred by your GP or community health nurse.

Age is an issue of mind over matter. If you don't mind, it doesn't matter.

— Mark Twain

You may get one to three days per week at one or more centers, transport and meals are provided, plus access to some services like physiotherapy, chiropody and hairstyling.

This helps to give structure to the week, provides a nutritious balanced meal and some social interactions to elderly people living alone.

H.S.E. FUNDING PACKAGES

The Home Care Package.

Home care support packages are largely offered to older people who are already using existing core community services.

This is available to those requiring medium to high caring supports in order to continue to live at home independently.

Each support package is tailored to each individual care needs, and is dependent on the individuals medical condition & level of care required, it is important to note that home care packages are designed to enhance rather than replace home support services already in the community.

A Care needs assessment is required and in the majority of cases is carried out by your local Public health nurse, she will assess your care needs and will determine with the client & or with the family how your needs would be most appropriately met.

For further information and an application form you will need to talk to your local Health Centre or Social worker. To find out more about this grant contact: www.hse.ie

The Department of Social and Family affairs also can assist.

FAIR DEAL NURSING HOME SUPPORT PACKAGE

The Fair Deal, or Nursing Home Support Scheme, was established in October 2009 as a means of funding long-term care for the elderly.

A Fair Deal: all you need to know

[Written by **Joanne McCarthy** www.irishhealth.com]

The Fair Deal *nursing home support scheme, which provides financial assistance to people in need of long-term nursing home care, came into effect yesterday. This means that people can apply to the HSE to seek financial support for the cost of their long-term care.*

How does the nursing home support scheme work?

Under the scheme, you will make a contribution towards the cost of your care and the State will pay the balance. Essentially, the State will pay the shortfall between what someone can afford to pay and the actual cost of nursing home care. This applies whether the nursing home is public, private or voluntary. Any person of any age who needs nursing home care can apply for the scheme.

What nursing homes are included in the scheme?

Public and voluntary nursing homes are included, and approved private nursing homes are also involved. Approved private nursing homes are homes that have agreed the price charged for care and are approved for the purposes of the scheme.

The HSE has a list of nursing homes to choose from, and a patient can choose any home from the list provided it has a place for you and it can cater for your particular needs.

Regardless of whether you choose a public or voluntary nursing home, you will pay your contribution and the HSE will pay the balance.

How do I avail of the scheme?

In order to avail of the scheme, you will need a financial assessment to determine your contribution to your care. You will also need a care needs assessment to identify whether or not you need long-term nursing home care.

How much do I contribute to my care?

In order to assess how much a person can afford to contribute, every applicant must undergo a financial assessment. This will examine your income and assets in order to work out what your contribution to care will be. The HSE will then pay the balance of your cost of care. For example, if the cost of your care was €1,000 and your weekly contribution was €300, the HSE will pay the weekly balance of €700.

What is included in the financial assessment?

The financial assessment will look at all of your income and assets. Income includes any earnings, pension income, social welfare benefits/allowances, rental income, income from holding an office or directorship, income from fees, commissions, dividends or interest, or any income which you have deprived yourself of in the five years leading up to your application. An asset is any material property or wealth, including property or wealth outside of the State. The assessment will not take into account the income of other relatives such as your sons or daughters.

How is my contribution calculated?

Having looked at your income and assets, the financial assessment will work out your contribution to care. **<u>You will contribute 80% of your assessable income and 5% of the value of any assets per annum</u>**. However, the first €36,000 of your assets, or €72,000 for a couple, will not be counted at all in the financial assessment. In the case of a couple, the assessment will be on the basis of half of the couple's combined income and assets.

Where your assets include land and property in the State, the 5% contribution based on such assets may be deferred. This means that the HSE will pay the money to the nursing home on the applicant's behalf and it will be collected after the applicant's death. This benefit, the nursing home loan, is optional, aimed at ensuring that the person doesn't have to sell assets such as their home during their lifetime. It can be repaid at any time but will ultimately fall due for repayment after your death. As well as this, the applicant's home will only be included in the financial assessment for the first three years of their time in care.

Every patient will keep a personal allowance of 20% of your income or 20% of the maximum rate of the state pension, whichever is the greater.

If the patient has a spouse or partner remaining at home, he or she will be left with 50% of the couple's income or the maximum rate of the state pension, whichever is the greater. No person will pay more than the cost of the care.

How will my care needs be assessed?

A care needs assessment will identify whether or not you need long-term nursing home care. Its purpose is to ensure that long-term nursing home care is necessary and is the right choice for you. The assessment will consider *whether you can be supported to continue living at home or whether long-term nursing home care is more appropriate.*

The care needs assessment will be carried out by appropriate healthcare professionals who are appointed by the HSE. An assessment may be completed at any time in a hospital or a community setting, such as your own home. The assessment will include consideration of the following:

- *Your ability to carry out the activities of daily living such as bathing, shopping, dressing and moving around*
- *The medical, health and personal social services being provided to you or available to you both at the time of the carrying out of the assessment and generally*
- *The family and community support available to you*
- *Your wishes and preferences.*

Assessment may include a physical examination by a healthcare professional.

What is the next step?

Once your care and financial assessments have been processed the HSE will write to you. Firstly, it will advise you of your contribution to care and whether you are eligible for State support. Secondly, if you have applied for the nursing home loan, it will also advise you about your eligibility for this. Thirdly, it will provide you with a list of nursing homes to choose from. The list will include public nursing homes, voluntary nursing homes and approved private nursing homes, as mentioned above. Your choice of nursing home is not connected in any way to the level of your contribution to care.

How does it apply to people currently in a public or private nursing home?

People who are already living in a public nursing home will continue to contribute to their care on the same basis as they have been. If a person is already resident in a private nursing home, they will continue with the existing arrangement or they may avail of the new scheme if they wish.

How do I apply for the scheme?

In order to apply for the scheme, you must be ordinarily resident in Ireland. This means that you have been living here for at least a year or that you intend to live here for at least a year. A standard application form can be obtained from the HSE's website, *www.hse.ie*. Or *www.careformumanddad. com*" Guide to the Fair Deal" and The Application form for Fair Deal

Your local nursing homes support office is available to help you fill in the application form or answer questions about your application. When you have completed the form, send it to the office for your area. There are 18 regional offices around the country, the contact details of which are available at *http://hse.ie/eng/services/Find a Service/Older People Services/ nhss*.

Information is also available from the HSE at 1850 24 1850, from Monday to Saturday between 8am and 8pm. The HSE is advising anyone who is concerned or confused about the scheme to contact with their local health office and ask to speak to a nursing home support scheme officer or to contact the HSE information line.

FAMILY CARERS

There are three different schemes available to assist carers:

The Carers Allowance

This is a means-tested payment for carers on low income, who look after people in need of full time care & attention. If you meet all the payments eligibility criteria then you may be entitled to this allowance from the Department of Family & Social Affairs.

The Carers Benefit

This payment may be awarded to those people who leave the workforce in order to care for someone in need of full time care & attention. People in receipt of this Benefit are allowed to work 15 hours per week and still claim their allowance.

The Respite Grant

Certain carers may be eligible for a Respite Grant an annual payment by the Department of Social & Family Affairs, which can be used by carers as they wish. All Carers in receipt of the Carer's Benefit and the Carers Allowance will automatically receive the Grant. Others carers providing full time care may also be eligible for the grant, providing you fulfill certain criteria. **You must be caring for a person on a full time bases for at least 6 months and must not be working or participating in training or education courses for more than 15 hours per week.**

Charities Supporting Elderly Care

Carers Association,

Offer training, advice and support for family care givers.

There are grants and other services available if you choose to take on the role of a family carer to care for your elderly parents.

The carers association is an amazing resource to help you gain knowledge, social interaction with other family carers and be aware of the toll this takes on your health and time and helps you to survive this very difficult role.

Friends of the Elderly

Visiting elderly people who feel alone is the most important work carried out by Friends of the Elderly. Their abiding motto is; "above all we need love."

They now have 400 volunteers visiting elderly people in their homes or in nursing homes or hospital.

Elderly people are generally referred to them by social workers, GPs, community nurses, concerned neighbours or relatives.

They then do their best find a volunteer in your area with a view to developing a close and sincere friendship.

The volunteer also becomes the link between their old friend and the activities of Friends of the Elderly, informing them of organised events in which they can take part in like visits to the theatre, concerts, park walks, day excursions and short holidays.

Care Local and Cross Care

Are working to reduce loneliness and support independence in Dublin and have a few programmes like **Befrienders**, who will visit an elderly person

Age is a matter of feeling, not of years.
— George William Curtis

in their area each week for an hour and just bring them up to date on local news over a cup of tea, they also have **Plate Pals** who sit with patients in hospital and help them eat their meals, as often in hospital, meals are served and then collected by catering staff and nursing staff will not be aware that the elderly person hardly touched their meal.

"This is why when our clients are in hospital our carers spend several hours daily with their client and assist with meals and toileting and companionship, as the nursing staff are so sh ort handed that patients have to wait far too long to be assisted in going to the toilet and this is distressing and results in accidents and people losing their dignity."

Age Action Ireland

Have many services to support positive aging and advocacy of the elderly. They also have a great service called

Care and Repair

The Care & Repair Programme was established by Age Action to carry out minor repairs for older and vulnerable people and to provide a befriending service. The programme is currently delivered directly by Age Action volunteers and staff in Cork, Dublin and Galway.

In addition to this some twenty local community entities (or Franchise Partners) work to deliver the service with the support of Age Action throughout the country. This outreach is continuing to be developed.

The vision of the Age Action Care and Repair Programme is to enable older and vulnerable people to remain in their own homes, in their own communities, living as independently as possible, through the improvement of their housing conditions and their level of comfort and security.

To achieve this vision, Care and Repair has developed and provides a range of practical repair and care services for older and vulnerable people. These include:

Small repairs service
Home Visiting/Befriending Service
Trades Referral Service
Quote Check Service
Daily Contact Service

To ARRANGE TO HAVE A JOB DONE? LO-CALL: 1890 369 369 (Ireland only)

Alzheimer's Society is a great resource centre for families who have had a parent diagnosed with Alzheimer's they offer support to families and the main caregiving spouses.

They can help with weekly visits to offer some hours respite for the family care giver, a network to gain support advice and best tips on how to manage day to day caring of a person with Alzheimer's or Dementia.

"Wisdom comes with winters"

— Oscar Wilde

Alone

ALONE is an independent charity that provides homes, friendship, and a crisis response service for older people in need.

As a grass-roots organisation they believe that each member of the community has a role to play in supporting and caring for older people. They work in partnership with many organisations across the public and private sectors to offer support to those older people who are most in need.

In 2011 calls to ALONE for help and advice were up 50% on the same period in 2010 and up 125% on 2009. At any one time they are supporting 330 individuals.

In an environment of ongoing reductions in state services and general cutbacks ALONE remains committed to maintaining a consistent quality of service and to extending their services where necessary. www.alone.ie

ALONE SERVICES

BEFRIENDING

Alone offers companionship to older people who would otherwise be lonely or isolated. Through weekly visits a team of 130 trained and Garda-vetted befriending volunteers provide companionship to the people they visit and help them to integrate in their community and pursue their life-goals. Staff support volunteers and offer advice and advocacy on issues such as housing, health, transport, safety, life-long learning and leisure.

SUPPORTIVE HOUSING

They provide affordable accommodation in life-long tenancies for older people who are homeless or at risk of becoming homeless. ALONE maintains more than 90 homes at various locations throughout Dublin city. Residents are supported by professional staff that develops individual support plans, which focus on maximising their independence for as long as possible. They are renovating all of their properties to ensure that they meet the highest age-friendly standards.

COMMUNITY RESPONSE

They also operate an outreach service for older people in emergency situations or suffering from hardship. They can directly help and or advocate for older people in poverty or experiencing difficulties with housing or health issues. Last year they assisted more than

1,000 older people in fuel poverty through a very successful partnership with Bord Gáis.

SOCIAL PROGRAMME
The ALONE social programme includes large and small events to suit a range of interests. They organise four seasonal dinner dances with 150- 200 older people enjoying each event. Recent smaller outings included trips to the theatre and the Botanic Gardens. Last year's annual summer holiday took a group of 40 to a Kilkenny hotel for a weekend. Their weekly cinema club has been running for 10 years, bringing 25 older people out to a classic film, followed by a light meal.

CAMPAIGNING AND INFORMATION
ALONE campaigns to keep the issues that affect their service users on the public agenda, through press releases, their website and social media. For many years, volunteers have offered a very popular interactive schools presentation, introducing students to the issues that face vulnerable older people and the work of ALONE. They can also offer presentations to community groups and businesses.

For all resources and contacts for all services mentioned plus international services go to my website www.careformumanddad.com

CHAPTER 3

Einy, Meany, Miny, MO?

How do I know which is best suited to our situation?
Pros and Cons of available services and schemes.

In the chapter "The good old days", I outlined the core services, grants and packages available in Ireland.

"I will love you always. When this red hair is white, I will still love you. When the smooth softness of youth is replaced by the delicate softness of age, I will still want to touch your skin. When your face is full of the lines of every smile you have ever smiled, of every surprise I have seen flash through your eyes, when every tear you have ever cried has left its mark upon your face, I will treasure you all the more, because I was there to see it all. I will share your life with you, Meredith, and I will love you until the last breath leaves your body or mine."

— Laurell K. Hamilton, A Lick of Frost

In the UK, USA and Europe due to larger populations and greater needs they have more comprehensive services and infrastructure than currently available in Ireland.

They have planned retirement villages, communities and sheltered housing for those who can manage alone but like the idea of help being close at hand and a sense of community, yet maintaining their autonomy

Retirement Community and Purpose Built Sheltered Housing

Downsizing is quite a good idea, especially when the family have all grown and moved on people often find the family home is too big to maintain, to heat, to clean etc.

Downsizing especially in a boom property market is a great move as you can maximize your profits from the sale giving you a good nest egg, which can then be reinvested.

Selling the family home and moving into a one or two bedroomed flat /bungalow is a good idea, however thinking further ahead and getting a new flat or home in a special retirement community or sheltered housing programme which has been specifically designed for people in their golden years and will have wider doors, to accommodate reduced mobility aids like Zimmer frames and wheelchairs.

Spacious wet room type bathrooms and emergency call bells. A dedicated warden is always on duty, so of you have difficulties you can get help fast, yet maintain your privacy and be able to live a normal life.

Added benefits can be you could develop new friends on site, making social interaction easy and accessible if you choose to join in.

There are now a few retirement villages in Ireland and some have attached nursing home and day care facilities plus other services.

I have also found in the Costa Del Sol Spain there are many such properties as people do fair better in the warm weather, the draw back is distance from family and friends.

Some I have seen have a rental option, which means you can try for a year and rent your home out as this gives you a chance to see if you will like it.

http://www.retirementservices.ie

The disadvantage is giving up your home and all it's memories, having a smaller place so there is no room for family visiting with children. If you leave it until you really need to move you are generally too old to face a move and it would cause more heartache than happiness.

You may be like my Mother and just hate the thought of people encouraging her to join in she prefers the company of family, her TV, books and dog.

Small Fully Staffed Group Nursing Homes

In the USA they are now trying to do a group type home instead of large purpose built nursing homes, where 4-6 residents have their rooms and bathrooms and share dining and communal space with a couple of carers on duty at all times.

This is a much better model than a nursing home and these homes could be built in small clusters as part of community development and planners can allocate space for these developments and ensure they are near all local amenities.

This helps share the cost of care among residents and they have a purpose built home with modern conveniences and designed for senior residents who may have compromised mobility.

Having a small team of familiar care staff, catering and social interaction in a safe and healthy environment, plus your own private space seems to me a far better solution than large impersonal nursing homes.

The disadvantage is you still have to give up your home, your local community and perhaps move to an area you are unfamiliar with and don't like.

You have to leave neighbours and friends behind and the familiar surroundings you may have been used to for the past 40-50- years.

You can't have family stay over or really have them visit with children in any large numbers, as this is a house not a large building like a nursing home where there is lots of space for visitors.

Family Carers

This is the perfect solution for all parents or spouses; they can have their loved, trusted and familiar family member (son, daughter or spouse) to provide for all their care needs.

They remain in their own home, mostly, however in some cases they may need to move in with a son or daughter who will become the" family Carer "if it is more convenient.

There was a trend a few years ago to add a granny flat onto a suitable property and have your Mum or both parents live in a small purpose built unit either attached to your main home or in the grounds.

This way you still have your space but caring and providing meals and help with appointments is much more convenient.

The disadvantage is not to the person needing care but to the Carer.

Spouses looking after each other is very difficult and does have a very heavy toll on the caring spouses health (see the stories below)

We are very familiar with our family members and this can lead to abuse even by the most upstanding members of society.

There are many form of abuse and in families abuse can be not listening, shouting, making your parent feel like a burden, withholding of pension is also abuse and it does not always have to be physical.

A story in "Emmerdale" the TV soap highlighted this with the church pastor and his elderly father.

Family Carers are always on duty they can't go home after their shift, it is very tedious, exhausting and in many cases not appreciated.

Elderly parents can be domineering, manipulative and also abusive. They can use guilt to get their own way.

I have also witnessed threats of cutting family out of their will if their wishes were not complied with.

With dementia and Alzheimer's it is much harder to be patient with your own family members than it is for a carer, as blood relatives we have learned to push each other's buttons.

Even with allowances it is not an easy role to do day in and day out.

Being a family carer can seriously affect your health and relationships.

You put your needs, your husband and children's needs all second and this is very unhealthy.

Family carers' surveys have found they have very high rates of depression and stress related illnesses.

PERSONAL STORIES

I would like to share with you a few stories where the main carer was the spouse and in all 3 of these cases died suddenly and without any pre existing conditions.

All 3 were men, who were looked after by their strong, healthy and youthful wives,

The gentlemen were social and young in outlook, not sick weak old men.

2 had Parkinson's and one had dementia.

Greif struck after the sudden loss of their Mothers (and wives) I was contacted by their grieving families to implement care at short notice for three lovely gentlemen. These gentlemen were also now faced with adjusting to a new life, firstly as a widower and secondly to be cared for by "a stranger".

Thankfully all adjusted and felt happy with their carers who were specially selected for them, at this special time.

Helping people especially in these sad circumstances is very rewarding as you watch them rebuild a new life as a widower.

Unfortunately, all of these gentlemen have since passed.

When they passed sadly and unexpectedly, they were not in the care of Casa A Carers. One was admitted into hospital and was recovering well as his carer was in attendance daily, he was taken off his intravenous drip, and was waiting for the Occupational Therapist to asses his swallow reflex and give instructions on re -feeding, however on the weekend they don't work and nursing staff were given no feeding instructions, so he was not given anything by mouth, by Tuesday morning he sadly and unexpectedly passed away.

The other two were transferred to nursing homes to avail of the fair deal scheme, we had cared for them respectively for 2 and 4 years. They were both in good health and very well, naturally they were upset at having to leave home, however within 6 months shockingly both were dead.

I have many more stories of patients doing well at home then dying in a very short space of time without any real reason once they are transferred to either the hospital or nursing home.

The stories are all true and not just because I am biased towards home care.

I am sure there are many people who do well in nursing homes however obviously the clients who contact me definitely want to remain at home.

Day Centers

In Ireland they do have many Day Centers where transport is provided, a cooked meal and some social interaction on weekdays It is up to the local health care professional to allocate places and some people manage to get one day per week, others up to 3 days as part of helping with loneliness and care needs.

Disadvantages are people sometimes don't feel well enough to go, they don't want to go as they need to get up extra early and rush to get ready, also when it is very cold outside, they want to stay close to the fire.

If they don't go they will be alone all day as no service will be provided during the day center hours also they may then have to organize food for themselves.

This means they have reduced their ability to choose how to spend their days and have to go with the flow dictated by someone else.

Home Help and Home Care Attendants

There is also the Home Help and Home care attendants service and you may get assistance with light housekeeping, running small errands and basic care needs such as getting out of bed, getting meals delivered, having a shower, and being put to bed.

Disadvantages are you can't choose the time that suits you; it's when they can slot you in, although the home helps are doing their best they just don't have time to chat with the patients, as they must do what they have to do in the short time given. Many elderly people start to feel like a side of beef being pushed around to suit someone else timetable they are not getting the companionship and time they desire.

Hourly Private Home Care

Private home care provides an hourly service and is usually paid for by the individual. This means you have more freedom of choice to decide when it best suits you to have care services and for how many hours.

They can also do light housekeeping, cook a meal and get some shopping for you.

They also cover nights and any time you want by arrangement.

You may be able to get a **Home Care Package** to assist with the costs of private home care. Alternatively you may be awarded a number of hours supplied by a private company and paid for by the HSE.

Private home care allows you the freedom to remain at home and have just the right amount of care at the times suitable for you to suit your needs and preferences, carers can assist with shopping, meal preparation, housekeeping as well as assistance with bathing and dressing.

Disadvantages

I can't think of any disadvantage except you will have to pay for private care. Or some of it

Personal Live in Home Care

This has been a growing trend since 2005 now there is a proliferation of home care service providers.

As with the explosion of growth of nursing homes since 1995, some operators are in the business purely for profit.

Casa Carers created a customized model of professional, personalized and socially interactive, live in care in 2007. The trend at that time, by the few operators providing care services were predominantly hourly care services or night cover.

We set out to create affordable packages to allow people to stay at home with a full time "LIVE IN" personal carer, and to provide a living plan which included socialization, mental stimulation, companionship and bespoke packages for each individuals need, budget and desires.

Having a live in personal carer means the family can rest easy knowing their Mum or Dad is being well looked after, the whole family have a relationship with the carer and the agency.

The stress and worry is lifted from the family and indeed the person being cared for as they now have the continuity of the same carer(s) all the time.

This means a great deal to the person being cared for, as they still feel somewhat independent and in control of their own affairs and home.

Yet they have help on hand and don't need to bother the family or wait for community services like Home Help.

We have developed a customized model based on social interactive care, this means having the same personal carer a relationship of trust is built up and the person needing care can do almost anything they wish, travel, go for outings, hospital visits all because they have a personal carer.

Part of our personalized service, is to improve the quality of life of our clients this would include little luxuries like getting a hand or foot massage plus daily routines like grooming, applying make up and painting their nails. We also encourage them to play stimulating mind games, crosswords, word search or memory cognition exercises plus provide security and companionship.

Alzheimer's and Dementia sufferers always thrive best with personal live in care.

Dementia sufferers thrive on the familiarity of their surroundings and constant care from the same person plus following their daily routines. This has proved to keep people afflicted with dementia more comfortable and contented.

Stress and agitation is very bad for anyone and more so with Alzheimer's or Dementia sufferers. They do very often get distressed in large groups and unfamiliar surroundings and this is when they are most likely to display aggressive and un- cooperative behaviours'.

This is possibly the most ideal form of care, and would be my choice and I am not advocating this because I run a personal Home Care service.

I run a Personal Home Care Service because this is my passion and is my personal choice in care.

In Ireland the HSE can award a home care package to subsides the cost of a live in service and you can then obtain a tax rebate of up to 41% of the remaining costs, up to a maximum of €55,000 per annum. This can mean care per week can be as low as a couple of hundred euros.

For many personal home care has allowed families to care for their Mum's and Dad's in a way that everyone benefits.

The families who come to us believe that personal home care is the best solution, and want the very best for their parent's final years.

For some personal care is a lifeline to maintain their independence, as not only elderly people need care we also provide care for clients with intellectual and physical disabilities, and have disorders such as Motor Neurons disease, Parkinson's, Multiple Sclerosis, Brain Injury/tumor, cerebral palsy to name just a few.

A few years ago we had a client who brought her sister home from hospital to die as she had cancer, her sister responded so well to treatment and being home she made a full recovery.

We also have had clients whose families were split on home care versus nursing home care and have brought home patients from nursing homes who thrived back at home and the family members who were opposed were converted when they saw how much better their mum was and how much happier she became again.

I have just had a client recently celebrate her 90th Birthday we brought her home from a nursing home 5 years ago. The family had put her in the home as they were instructed by the hospital that this would be the best solution when she broke her leg.

She was very unhappy and became very confused in the home asking daily to go home.

The family then contacted me to investigate the possibility of bringing her home. I truly believe she would not have lasted a year in the home, yet she has been happy and well cared for surrounded by her family and the same carer for years

Disadvantages

You have to provide a private room for your carer and all their meals whilst on duty, and still maintain the running cost of your home.

Or when a person is unable to remain in the home due to severe ill health and or needs active care round the clock the cost can become prohibitive.

Situations like palliative care, double incontinence, night wandering and disturbances.

Requiring two full time carers in these situations could be astronomical, however we can provide this for *€1,999 per week making it a short term viable option especially for Palliative Care.

*Prices correct Jan 2015

Nursing Homes

Nursing Homes up until about 8-10 years ago was the only place you could get full time care for your elderly Mum or Dad. And they were always the first recommendation of hospital and social workers as this was the trend.

If the doctors or healthcare team decided your Mum or Dad were no longer able to live unassisted then this was the only viable solution.

If you could afford it you went private and fees can be from €800 –€1,800 or higher per week.

Nursing homes are only a good choice if the person actually would like this arrangement and love the company, or their care needs have become so great and in order to remain at home they would need two carers 24/7 making it financially not manageable for some people.

Disadvantages are dementia sufferers are more open to being abused, they do not like crowds and lots of different staff large corridors are confusing and all this leads to distress and agitation which is treated by sedation and they then sit half comatose in a chair and are manageable.

Would you want this?

They will experience a general loss of advocacy; their personal choices are largely removed, as you need to follow the institutions routines.

Nursing homes like everywhere else usually don't have enough staff, in order to give you much one to one companionship.

Many people hate large groups, become depressed and withdrawn; feel isolated and not loved when place in a nursing home.

Like small children older people need love and affection, they want to chat and tell their stories. They have time now to take life at a leisurely pace, yet nursing homes are so regimented and the staff have no time to really chat or are encouraged to do so.

You are a number and on their shift their quota has to be fulfilled, they have x number of patients to wash, dress, feed and clean rooms and change incontinence pads. *This goes on like clockwork for their 12 hour shifts, leaving care workers drained and exhausted and if they are sensitive many carers feel unhappy and frustrated, as they know their patients want and need more from them.*

You may find other residents are disruptive, aggressive, destructive, noisy, and nosey. In general this place is not where you wish to be for lots of different reasons.

Many people agree to go to a nursing home as they don't want to be a burden on their children and have been convinced by others this is the best solution.

The Fair Deal in Ireland encourages them to avail of this deal to pay for their care costs and give over the money from their property to pay for their care.

"Personally, in my opinion this is not a fair deal, as you have lost the choice to stay in your own home. A fairer deal would be using equity from your homes to use for your care costs.

This way your home becomes like an insurance policy which we can cash in to help pay for our care costs."

Currently I am 55 years old whilst writing this book plus caring for my mother quite a lot recently, and running a home care service I am acutely aware of the fact someday my children may be planning my care.

Everything is getting more expensive and it is up to all of us, now to make sure that the taxes we have paid all our working lives is used for planning and providing the care we deserve and desire, when our turn comes!

Don't you agree?

SUMMARY

Care is a very personal choice and most people start with family members helping out during periods of crises.

I have been doing this fairly often recently, spending months with my mother whilst writing this book. I know realistically if her care needs increase or she continues to need more help on a daily basis, I can't continue and will need to suggest getting some help in as I live between Ireland and Spain and she lives in Scotland.

I also know I will be met with resistance as many families are when they come to me at first.

I also have a client whom we cover weekends for as her daughter is the main carer during the week and other sisters are taking turns at night. I know how difficult this is for her daughter as she has no life of her own and can't go on holidays as her mum will not go into a home for respite.

Being a family carer has to be the most difficult job, as it is definitely easier to care for a non-family member. Family carers very often suffer from stress related illness and burnout.

Nursing homes are far too institutionalized as they stand today and I have a vision for nursing homes where they truly feel like home with small groups, lots of your own stuff around, a welcoming personal living space, like a bed sitting room with your own TV and radio.

Where you can have the ability to make a cup of tea when you feel like it or get assistance immediately and have choices of what to eat and when with friends and family in a café like setting.

When nursing homes become like this then I would be less averse to being in one.

I realize now that care needs to be discussed, planned for and agreed long before it becomes urgent and essential.

I think knowing what I know today I would have had this discussion with my parents when they were in their early seventies, and as a family discussed everything and agreed to a specific plan.

As it concerned something that "may happen" at some point in the future, the stress of this conversation would be largely removed.

However, this is not a subject many people want to discuss at any age.

I realize now, talking about it brings home the reality that our lives are not eternal and our mortality at some point will take over.

I truly hope, this book will help you and your loved ones at whatever stage you are at, to think and plan for what is the best solution for your family and yourselves using all the bonus resources I have included.

CHAPTER 4
Create your own DIY Will, Legally!

Bernadette Parte set up her own law firm in 2009 and in 2010 she was joined by Suzanne Cleary to become Parte and associates. They are based conveniently in Dublin City Center.

Her vision is to remain a small firm where they offer a very personalized service and her passion is taking care of the elderly and that is her specialization.

Building relationships and getting the best for their clients and their families is what drives her.

Bernadette Parte

Before establishing Parte & Associates in 2009, Bernadette qualified as a solicitor in 1996, representing both public bodies and private clients. She has advised on all aspects of the law that govern statutory functions of public bodies and in particular the law relating to mental health, nursing homes, food hygiene and pre-schools.

Bernadette has a particular interest in advising older people about their rights and entitlements and has extensive experience in the areas of estate planning, nursing home legislation, mental health law and wardship.

Bernadette was recently re-appointed by the Mental Health Commission to advocate and advise people who are involuntarily detained in approved centres under the Mental Health Acts 2001-2008. She is a member of the Solicitors for the Elderly in Ireland, the Health and Safety Lawyers Association of Ireland, the Irish Mental Health Lawyers Association and the Dublin Solicitors and Bar Association. Bernadette is a Notary Public having being appointed by the Chief Justice of Ireland. She is also a regular contributor to the Senior Times' website.

Why you must have a will

Would you be surprised to know that a staggering 60% of us have not made a Will?

So why would you be reluctant to make a Will, even though most people will agree it is an extremely important document?

It seems that we do not want to face the reality of our own deaths and more so the emotional complications that may arise for the people involved.

We don't make Wills because:

- We are afraid of upsetting people in our family;
- We are afraid about what will happen to our children when we are gone, especially if we have young children or children with drug problems, drink problems or dependent children with, for example, an intellectual disability;
- We are fearful of dying;
- We feel uncertain about what comes next – is there an afterlife? What will it be like?
- We fear that it is a morbid thing to do and we will be 6 feet under in no time.

All of these issues may come to the fore when you consider making a Will. I can say however that I have been making Wills for almost 20 years and to date only one of my clients have died; the others remain fit and healthy!

When I developed my own practice, I wanted to focus on the needs of older and vulnerable people to let them know what legal protections they can avail of, such as having a valid Will, an Enduring Power of Attorney, a robust contract of care for those who employ a carer, either in their own home or in a nursing home, so that they are empowered and their dignity protected.

1. YOU DECIDE

The first most important reason why you should make a Will is so that YOU DECIDE who gets what you have worked for throughout your life. If you don't put your wishes – your will – in writing, the laws of intestacy apply and often that can lead to unwanted consequences. Most people want to benefit their families but it is important to do this in a structured way, so that tax is minimized, and so that your wishes can be followed.

A Will is an excellent device for tax planning. By way of example, a mother leaves a house worth €250,000 to her son and daughter in law in her Will. Her son receives his share of the house completely tax free as – at the moment – a parent can leave up to €250,00 to a child without their having to pay inheritance tax.

However, the daughter in law can only receive €16,604 tax free. So she must now pay inheritance tax of €32,500 on her inheritance from her mother in law.

This is a large sum of money for people to come up with and while the Revenue Commissioners do allow people to pay tax in installments, over say 5 years, the amount still has to be paid.

If that mother had instead left the house to her son only in her Will, he would have paid no tax, and he could then transfer the house into the joint names of himself and his wife with no tax payable. That's a simple example of a tax saving in a Will.

Making a Will also saves you money because the process of Probate is less costly and quicker than administering an intestate estate.

When you make a Will, you also get to choose who will administer your estate and it is very important that you pick people who are organised, willing to do the job, and able for the task.

We all know people whose homes are perfect, their dishcloths lined up, everything neat and tidy. And most of us also know people for whom tidiness is not a priority and whose cupboards are bulging. I suggest when it comes to your executors that you choose people who fall into the first category!

2. WILL SHOULD BE VALID AND REFLECT CURRENT CIRCUMSTANCES

It is not enough to have a Will: it must be valid. If you have a Will that is deemed invalid, you will be deemed to have died intestate.

What do I mean by valid? Firstly, you must be over 18 (or married) and of sound disposing mind. Secondly, you must sign it at the bottom and your signature must be witnessed by two people, in the presence of the testator (person making Will) and in the presence of each other.

It is very important that you do not invalidate a gift in a Will by having a beneficiary witness your signature.

You don't have to go to a solicitor to make a Will but be very careful of getting the formalities right if you do not. A recent case involving the estate of the writer, John O'Donoghue, the author of 'Anam Cara' and other books about Celtic wisdom is a prime example of how crucial it is to follow the formalities when making a Will.

John died in 2008 but only recently has his family been able to distribute his estate worth approximately €2 million. He made two Wills, one in 1998, with the benefit of legal advice, and another in 2001, which he wrote himself and had his signature witnessed by his mother and one of his brothers.

Unfortunately, the second Will (which revoked the first) had numerous problems with it. It was undated, it was witnessed by his mother and brother who were to benefit under the Will, it was imprecise in its terms and was rendered invalid by the High Court due to uncertainty. It ultimately meant that John O'Donoghue died intestate, his mother inheriting his entire estate.

What's wrong with that, you might ask. Leaving aside the expense of the High Court case which had to interpret the Will, the O'Donoghue family have inherited an enormous inheritance tax bill and burden.

If you have made a Will, it should reflect your current circumstances, especially if you have experienced major life events, such as marriage, divorce, death of a spouse, ill health.

I recently met a woman who queried why she would need a Will. She told me that she had been married but separated from her husband for the past 30 years. She described how her father had had to travel over to England to rescue her and her young daughters from her violent spouse. She thought he now lives in America and had another family.

She was not divorced and nor was she formally separated from her husband. She had not made a Will.

I explained to her that her husband was entitled to one third of her estate and that if she did not make a Will, the administrators of her estate would be obliged to try to track down that husband to advise him of his entitlement to this share in her estate.

On the other hand, if she made a Will, leaving her estate to her daughters, and nothing to her husband, he would have to challenge the Will to claim his legal right share. That is a far harder task than being handed something on a plate and unfortunately we all know that some people no problem about taking something that they may have no moral right to. In fact, they are just the people who will come out of the woodwork.

3. MAKING A WILL CAN HELP AVOID FAMILY DISPUTES

Talking about Wills and Probate often conjures up in people's minds family conflict. Everyone is aware of someone left out of a Will, or the hardship caused by the fact that no Will was ever made.

Difficulties often arise when it comes to a family business. In a Will, you can make provision for who will take over the reins of the business and avoid costly litigation about what your intentions were. Also, a 90% reduction in inheritance tax relief may apply to businesses that are transferred on death provided that the business is transferred properly with an awareness of the law in this area.

However, when no provision is made, here is an example of what can happen:

A couple ran a family business for many years, and their sons joined them in the business when they became adults, working for years at a lower wage because they were due to take over the business from their parents in time. Their parents intended to make a Will leaving the business to their sons, and the remainder of their assets to their two daughters. Unfortunately, both parents died quite suddenly within a short spell of each other, and neither had made a Will.

Under the rules on intestacy, the four children were entitled to an equal quarter share in their parents' entire estate. To realize their share, the daughters insisted that the business be sold. This meant that the brothers now had to work with the new owners, and negotiate their wages. It also resulted in the brothers and sisters having a falling out and no longer talking to each other.

Sometimes even when one makes a Will, unforeseen consequences arise which again may lead to family strife. Some people do not care about what happens after they are gone, but most people do not want to leave behind them a legacy of hurt and broken relationships.

That was the concern of a woman who appeared on a BBC programme called "Can't Take It With You". She had four daughters, all of whom had children except for her youngest daughter. She was keen to leave a little extra to this youngest daughter but her husband was concerned that this would cause problems and hurt feelings. Gerry Robinson, who presented the programme, suggested that the family meet to have a discussion about the mother's wishes. It turned out that the three older daughters were completely understanding of their mother's wish to leave something extra to their youngest sister. This was in the context where the mother had helped out her daughters when they had children with babysitting and all the other things that mothers do. The mother was terminally ill and was aware that she would not be around to help her youngest daughter out in a similar way, which is why she wanted to leave something extra to this daughter. Both parents were massively relieved when this was sorted out, knowing that their children understood their wishes.

Also, problems can arise if you are in a non-traditional family. If a Will is not made, assets will pass to next of kin and not to a person you may have lived with for many years. Even under the new

Cohabitation legislation, no automatic succession rights apply and an application to Court must be brought to establish one's rights.

CONCLUSION

So to conclude, I hope that I have convinced you of the need to make a Will - or review your Will if you haven't looked at it for sometime - because it allows you to decide who gets what you have worked for throughout your life, it reflects your current circumstances, and it is one of the most loving things that you can do for your family.

LEGAL HEALTH CHECK

What is a legal health check?

A lot of people do not check these crucial matters until it is too late, leaving their loved ones to sort out problems in their wake. But taking preventative action now can save a lot of unnecessary trouble and expense later on.

What does a legal health check involve?

There are four steps in a legal health check:

Collect all your important papers. Even putting those papers together in one place can prevent future difficulty. Knowing that one is missing is also important and may give you the opportunity to remedy it.

Solicitor analyses your questionnaire. Having completed your questionnaire, we will analyze it to establish if there are gaps or inconsistencies in how you believe your affairs currently stand.

Recommendations will be made to improve your legal health, for example, if your will is out-of-date or invalid or if the bank's name is still on the title to your house.

Action plan. Action can then be taken to help guard your family and your future.

Preparing a Contract of care for a Nursing Home

A **Contract of Care** is agreed between you and the nursing home. This contract sets out the terms that are to govern your care and welfare and must include details of the services to be provided and the fees to be charged. It must be provided to every resident within two months of admission to the nursing home. The Code of Practice for Nursing Homes states that the contract should cover:

- ✓ The services to be provided to the resident;
- ✓ The level of fees, time and method of payment, whether in advance or in arrears;
- ✓ Extra services and appliances that are charged separately (this cannot include "essential" services);
- ✓ A procedure for increasing fees when necessary;
- ✓ Provision for review of placement;
- ✓ The personal items that a person may bring to the home and those that the home will provide;
- ✓ Arrangements for the care of pets (where allowed);
- ✓ Extra services and appliances that are charged separately (this cannot include "essential" services);
- ✓ Terms under which the resident may vacate the accommodation temporarily (e.g., for holidays or admission to hospital)
- ✓ The circumstances in which a resident can be asked to leave;
- ✓ The procedure on either side for terminating the arrangement or giving notice of changes;
- ✓ Statement of insurance cover;
- ✓ Provision for the observance of religious beliefs;
- ✓ The procedure on the death of a resident;
- ✓ The arrangement for holidays.

A comprehensive nursing review of the care of each resident should be undertaken by the nursing home at least every six months.

You may not be charged any more than the amount as agreed in the contract of care. This means that there can be no further separate charges for

> ➤ Bed and board,
> ➤ Nursing care appropriate to the level of dependency,
> ➤ Incontinence wear and bedding,
> ➤ Laundry service and aids and appliances necessary to assist a dependent person with the activities of daily living.

A special service or item of equipment must be the subject of a separate agreement between you and the nursing home and must be set out in the contract of care.

I have written a very comprehensive guide called "A Legal Guide for Older People" I have provided this as a Free Bonus Resource which you can download from the website.

All my details are there and you can contact me for any further information you may require.

Note ** We also have FREE Bonus Guides "Questions to ask when considering a Nursing Home" "Questions to ask before considering Home Care"

CHAPTER 5
Renovations, Equipment and Funding

Thankfully there are grants available to make alterations to your home to make them more age friendly.

Things we don't think about are wider doorways, grab rails, ramps to enter rather than or in addition to steps, wider shower or wet rooms, which can accommodate a wheelchair. Stair lifts, hoists and mechanical aids for ease of movement.

If we think about this parents of young children also need ramps and wider doorways for prams, so why don't Architects start designing homes which can be adaptable easily for babies, and people with disabilities and save costs in the long term.

The following information has been taken from the HSE and Citizens advice websites. Full information and resources are also available on www.care-for-mum-and-dad.com

The Housing Aid for Older Persons Scheme is used to improve the condition of an older person's home. In general, this scheme is aimed at people 60 years of age and above. *However, if there is a case of genuine hardship the local authority may give assistance to people less than 60 years of age.*

The Housing Aid for Older Persons Scheme replaced the Essential Repairs Grant administered by the local authorities and the Special Housing Aid for the Elderly administered by the Health Service Executive (HSE).

Rules

Local authorities vary as regards what type of work they will grant aid under the scheme. You should check with your own local authority to see which types of work its scheme will cover.

The type of work that is grant aided can include some or all of the following:

> *Structural repairs or improvements*
> *Re-wiring, repair or replacement of windows and doors*
> *The provision of water, sanitary services and heating*
> *Cleaning and painting*
> *Radon remediation*
> *Re-wiring and any other repair or improvement work considered necessary.*

Many older people may be eligible for the Scheme. However, priority will be given to people on the basis of financial need.

The grant can be paid to people in:

Owner-occupied housing

Houses being purchased from a local authority under the Tenant Purchase Scheme.

Priority applicants

Your application will be prioritised based on medical need. Highest priority will be given to a person who is terminally ill or where alterations/adaptations would facilitate your discharge from hospital or the continuance of care in your own home.

Occupational therapy report

When the local authority receives your application, it may request an Occupational Therapist's (OT) assessment. The local authority can arrange for an OT assessment. Alternatively, you can employ an OT to carry out an assessment and get back up to €200 as part of the total grant (up to the maximum you are entitled to).

Means test

The Housing Aid for Older Persons Scheme is a means-tested grant. This means that your total household income is assessed to find out if you qualify for the grant and at what level of assistance.

Household income is:

Property owner's (or tenant's) and spouse's/partner's annual gross income in the previous tax year

The following is not taken into account when calculating your household income:

€5,000 for each member of the household aged up to 18 years

€5,000 for each member of the household aged between 18 and 23 years and in full-time education or on a FÁS apprenticeship

€5,000 where the person to whom the grant relates is being cared by a relative on a full-time basis

Child Benefit

Family Income Supplement

Domiciliary Care Allowance

Respite Care Grant

Carer's Benefit and Carer's Allowance (if the carer's payment is made in respect of the person to whom the grant relates)

Tax clearance

If you get a grant of more than €10,000 you must have a valid Tax Clearance Certificate. If you intend to pay more than €650 to a contractor, you must get your contractor to submit his/her C2/Tax Clearance Certificate to the local authority.

Payment of a second grant

It is possible to get a grant under the Housing Aid for Older Persons Scheme a second time if your needs have substantially changed over time.

Starting the work

The grant will not be paid if you start work before the grant is approved. However, it is expected that the work will start within 6 months of your grant approval.

Rates

The maximum grant available under the Housing Aid for Older Persons Scheme is €10,500, which may cover 100% of the cost of works.

100% of the approved cost of works is available to those with annual household incomes of less than €30,000 and tapering to 30% for those with annual household incomes of €54,001 to €65,000.

Housing Aid for Older Persons Scheme:

Maximum Yearly Household Income	% of costs	% of costs Maximum Grant
Up to €30,000	100%	€10,500
€30,000 – €34,000	90%	€9,450
€34,001 – €38,000	80%	€8,400
€38,001 – €42,000	70%	€7,350
€42,001 – €46,000	60%	€6,300
€46,001 – €50,000	50%	€5,250
€50,001 – €54,000	40%	€4,200
€54,001 – €65,000	30%	€3,150
Over €65,000		No Grant Payable

The maximum grant levels will increase in line with the building cost index on an annual basis. This will protect the value of the grant into the future. However, income bands for the purposes of means testing will also be amended annually in line with wage inflation.

Adapting a home for an older or disabled person

Adapting your home may become necessary, as you grow older. You may also need to adapt your home if you or a family member has a disability.

Common alterations to make a home suitable for someone with a disability or limited mobility include:

> *Widening doorways and passageways*
> *Moving light switches, door handles, doorbells and entry phones to convenient heights*
> *Installing grab rails for support*
> *Adapting bathroom facilities (for example, raised toilet, back rest against the toilet cistern, level deck shower, bath with hoist, hand basin at appropriate height)*
> *Locating bathroom or bedroom facilities at ground-floor level*
> *Installing ramps to avoid using steps*
> *Ensuring that external approaches such as paths or drives have a firm, level surface*
> *Installing a stair lift or elevator*
> *Specialised furniture, like adjustable beds or support chairs*
> *Setting up alert devices for the deaf and hard of hearing*

In case of fire or other emergency, it is important that exits should always be accessible and that you do not rely entirely on mechanical means (such as a lift) to get out

Planning to adapt your home

Before making changes to your home you can consult an occupational therapist (OT) who will assess your daily living needs and advise on adaptations to your home. You can contact an OT through the community care section of your Local Health Office. Alternatively, you may wish to hire an OT privately, as there may be a waiting list for the public OT service. The Association of Occupational Therapists of Ireland (AOTI) publishes a listing of OTs in private practice, and if you get a grant for the adaptations you may be able to get back some of the costs of hiring the OT.

Other health professionals, such as public health nurses and physiotherapists, can also advise you on specialised equipment and home adaptations, based on both your short-term and long-term needs.

If you need to add a structure or an extra room, you may need planning permission.

Financial help

Adapting your home may be expensive, particularly if structural change is involved. There are several ways to lessen the financial burden:

If it would cost over €6,000 to make your home suitable for someone with a disability or a mental health difficulty, you may be eligible for a means-tested Housing Adaptation Grant for People with a Disability. The maximum grant is €30,000. Read more in our document on the Housing Adaptation Grant.

For more basic and cheaper alterations, such as grab rails, level access showers or chair-lifts, the Mobility Aids Grant Scheme (also means-tested) provides a maximum grant of €6,000. Read more in our document on the Mobility Aids Grant Scheme

The Housing Aid for Older Persons Scheme is used to improve the condition of an older person's home. The type of work covered includes structural repairs, re-wiring and upgrades to heating systems. Local authorities vary as regards what type of work they will grant aid. For information on what is covered in your area, contact your local authority.

You may qualify for a local authority home improvement loan to improve, repair or extend your home.

If you have a medical card or a long term illness card, you may be entitled to get essential items of equipment free of charge. First, a relevant professional, such as an occupational therapist or a physiotherapist, must assess you.

If you are paying for equipment needed for someone with a disability, you may be able to claim a VAT refund.

Sources of information

Assist Ireland provides impartial information on assistive technologies to help people with a disability to live independently. Tools and equipment range from simple items like lever taps on washbasins to more sophisticated devices such as computer screen-readers for people with visual impairments. Assist Ireland describes thousands of products and also provides factsheets describing specialised equipment and what you should consider when choosing it. There are several ways of contacting Assist Ireland with queries or feedback.

If you are visually impaired, deaf or hard of hearing, organisations like the National Council for the Blind in Ireland and Deafhear. ie offer advice on what you can do to make your home more manageable.

Age Action Ireland offers advice and information tailored to the needs of older people. It aims to improve their quality of life by enabling them to live independently in their own homes for as long as possible.

The Irish Wheelchair Association can provide information on alterations to make your home more wheelchair-friendly.

The National Disability Authority has produced a set of guidelines on accessibility entitled Building for Everyone. These guidelines show how buildings can be designed, built and managed so that they are accessible to everyone. You can download these guidelines from the NDA website.

Mobility Aids Grant Scheme

The Mobility Aids Grant Scheme was set up in 2007. The scheme provides grants for works designed to address mobility problems in the home. For example, the grant can be used for the purchase and installation of grab-rails, a level access shower, access ramps or a stair-lift.

The grant is primarily for older people but people with disability can also access the scheme.

You cannot apply for both the Mobility Aids Grant Scheme and the Housing Adaptation Grant for People with a Disability. However, you can withdraw your application for one scheme and submit a new application under the other.

Rules

The grant is available to people with a maximum household income less than €30,000.

The grant can be paid to people in:

> Owner occupied housing
> Houses being purchased from a local authority under the tenant
>   purchase scheme
> Private rented accommodation (the duration of your tenancy
>   can affect grant approval)

Accommodation provided under the voluntary housing Capital Assistance and Rental Subsidy schemes

Accommodation occupied by persons living in communal residences.

Your application will be prioritised based on medical need. Highest priority will be given to people who are terminally ill or where alterations/adaptions would facilitate discharge from hospital. When the local authority receives your application, it may request an Occupational Therapist's (OT) assessment. The local authority can arrange for an OT assessment, but under the new grant you can employ an OT to carry out an assessment and recoup up to €200 as part of the total grant up to the maximum you are entitled to.

Means test

The Mobility Aids Grant Scheme is a means-tested grant. This means your total household income is assessed to find out if you qualify for the grant and at what level of assistance.

Household income is:

Property owner's (tenant's in the case of private renting) and spouse's/partner's annual gross income in the previous tax year

The following is not taken into account when calculating your household income:

€5,000 for each member of the household aged up to 18 years

€5,000 for each member of the household aged between 18 and 23 years and in full-time education or a FAS apprenticeship

€5,000 where the person for whom the grant is for, is being cared by a relative on a full-time basis

Child Benefit

Family Income Supplement

Domiciliary Care Allowance

Respite Care Grant
Carer's Benefit and Carer's Allowance (if the carer's payment is made
in respect of the person for whom the grant is for)

Tax clearance

If you intend to pay more than €650 to a contractor, you must get your contractor to submit their C2/Tax Clearance Certificate to the local authority.

Starting the work to adapt your home

It is expected that the work will start within 6 months of your grant approval.

Rates

The maximum grant available will be €6,000 and may cover 100% of the cost of the work.

Apply to your local authority.

The Respite Care Grant

This is an annual payment made to carers by the Department of Social Protection. Carers can use the grant in whatever way they wish. You can use the grant to pay for respite care if you wish, but you do not have to do so. More information about respite care facilities is available.

In June of each year (usually on the first Thursday of the month), the Department of Social Protection pays the grant automatically to carers getting Carer's Allowance, Carer's Benefit, Domiciliary Care Allowance or Prescribed Relative's Allowance from the Department. Only one Respite Care Grant can be paid for each person getting care.

Rules

The grant is paid to people getting one of the payments mentioned above. It can also be paid to certain other carers providing full-time care. If you are not getting one of the above payments, you must be:

Aged 16 or over

Ordinarily resident in the State

Caring for the person on a full-time basis

Caring for the person for at least six months – this period must include the first Thursday in June

Living with the person being cared for or, if not, be contactable quickly by a direct system of communication (for example, telephone or alarm).

You do not qualify if you are working more than 15 hours per week outside the home, if you are getting an unemployment payment or if you are signing on for unemployment credits. You also do not qualify if you are living in a hospital, convalescent home or similar institution.

If you are caring for more than one person, a grant is paid for each of them.

Rates

A Respite Care Grant of €1,700 (June 2012) is paid once each year, usually on the first Thursday in June, for each person you are caring for. It is not taxable.

How to apply

If you are getting Carer's Allowance, Carer's Benefit, Domiciliary Care Allowance or Prescribed Relative's Allowance from the Department of Social Protection, you do not need to apply for the Respite Care Grant. It will be automatically paid to you in June.

If you are not getting one of these payments you should fill in an application form for the Respite Care Grant RCG 1 form.

If you are caring for two people or more you must fill in an RCG 1(a) Respite Care Grant form for each additional person and attach it to your completed RCG 1 form.

If you are not getting one of the above payments and you got the Respite Care Grant last year, you do not need to reapply this year using the RCG 1 form. If you got the grant last year, you will get a letter at the end of April this year from the Respite Care Section in the Department of Social Protection with a short questionnaire on the back. You must answer the questions on the back and return the letter to the Respite Care Section. A freepost envelope will be included with your letter. After you return the letter, the Department will use this and the information on file to reassess you for the Respite Care Grant.

Where to apply

You can get a Respite Care Grant application form from your Social Welfare Local Office or Citizens Information Centre.

Department of Social Protection

Respite Care Grant Section PO Box 10085 Dublin 2

Not living in Ireland?
** For information in your country visit our website for the free guides www.care-for-mum-and-dad.com

In Conclusion

Grants are available on a means tested basis; these are for renovation or urgent improvements for Health and Safety reasons.

Equipment can be supplied to private homes via the Public Health or Community Nurse, aids such as commodes, hoists, special chairs and hospital type beds.

The elderly often require security equipment like alarms linked to a service if they fall, panic buttons, push button door entry for visitors if they can't walk to the door.

People who have had strokes or with bad arthritis, may require special drinking and eating utensils.

Sometimes changing very simple things like converting a downstairs room into a bedroom and if possible adding an en-suite bathroom or getting a commode, can help or avoid major renovations upstairs.

Attention to lighting, as we age our sight diminishes so we need more lamps and brighter lights, so for economy use good energy saving bulbs, in order for your Mum and Dad not to worry about electricity bills.

Extra heating in a main room where they spend most of the time saves on keeping the whole house constantly warm.

Cosy blankets for covering legs and shoulders help keep them warm, however could also be a tripping hazard if they got up too fast.

Clear walk ways/ paths to the kitchen and bathroom, with less clutter can help with tripping, banging into furniture and prevent falls.

Rearranging the kitchen so things are within easy reach, plates can be heavy for an older person so having what they use every day to hand helps.

You must look for hazards all around, like loose rugs, threadbare carpets, old cables and sockets, a kettle too close to the stove.

For our free checklists and a complementary comprehensive guide to the UK and Ireland including suppliers visit our website www. care-for-mu-and-dad.com more countries like the US, Australia and New Zealand will be added in 2015/2016

Chapter 6
Difficult Conversations

Mary Rafferty is a Practitioner Mediator and Conflict Management Coach and her work focuses on helping people improve and transform relationships in their family and work life. In private practice since 2006, Mary brings her experience from two previous professional careers – education and social work – to a field she is passionate about – helping people to find ways towards greater harmony in their relationships at work, and ultimately better peace of mind. Mary is also the eldest child of a family of 5 and mother to two daughters aged 11 and 13. Mary's own mother died when she was just fifteen and as her father now approaches his later years, Mary has a deep understanding of the type of difficult conversations that troubles in family life can bring. Mary brings her personal and professional skills, abilities and philosophy to her work with people to build positive and supportive family relationships.

So far, this book has provided you with information and advice on many of the practicalities of supporting the care of your aging parent. While you are now well armed with ideas about what is and isn't workable, a key element of care is communicating about this with your elderly parent and between your siblings. This chapter will give you an overview of how best to manage this and cover key questions such as

- Where should I start
- How do I raise the issue of care needs with parent
- What should I say, how should I say things?
- What if they don't agree, see it as I do or resist my help?
- How do I convince them to take actions that are safer/ better for them
- How do I talk to my siblings about this
- What about if I or one of my siblings have had a difficult relationship with our parent in the past?

Why it can be difficult to have these conversations

Having a parent aging means that dealing with issues such as greater dependency, their finances and affairs, their health etc. is inevitable at some point. It can be tempting to just wait and let it happen and hope it all works out, or indeed to think that you know best and hope that they will slot into plans you have made for them. Equally, you might think that your parent is unwilling or reluctant to discuss their affairs with you, fearing they might impose or burden you unnecessarily. Furthermore, you might feel yourself that you don't wish to bother them with having to have such a heavy discussion until it's absolutely necessary.

It's essential to open up the lines of communication

This kind of thinking is understandable but can tend to be an excuse for not wanting to sit down and engage in what might be some difficult conversations with your parent. Yet a key aspect of talking to your parent make the necessary transitions required as they age is that

- They have a chance to talk about it and be fully involved and have ownership of the decisions that are made

- They have someone to talk to about their fears and anxieties who is willing to listen and be supportive
- They are reassured that you as their son or daughter are emotionally available and able to support them through the changes required

Talking to Your Parent:
Things to consider beforehand:

Consider first of all what outcome you want from talking to your parents and what your own intentions and motivations are. Get clear also on your own fears and needs. Realise that you too have needs and concerns around trying to juggle increased needs from your parents with the other demands in your life. Recognise these as well as any feelings of guilt you might have around feeling like this. Accept and acknowledge them and how they might be impacting on your conversation with your parent.

Put yourself in their shoes. Ask yourself, if you became ill tomorrow and unable to take care of yourself, what would be important to you? How hard would you find it to have to depend on someone else to look after you? How would it be for you to leave your home? What would be the difficult part of talking to your loved ones about these issues. Really try and get in touch with where your elderly parent might be emotionally with regards to such discussions. See if you can imagine the kind of anxiety, concern, insecurity that they might be feeling.

Consider also what might be feeding reluctance on their part to engage in such discussions. A key piece is an unwillingness to burden someone else with such issues. Having to come to terms with dependency is huge challenge and something that everyone needs time and patience with.

Getting started

See the opening of lines of communication as a process rather than event. Ideally start conversations about these topics at an early stage, when there are no pressing issues to be sorted.

First tentative steps might involve simply raising the topic in a casual way to test the waters and see how they react. You might start by talking in a general sense e.g. commenting about some local scenario where an elderly parent had to have home care or go into residential care and how that might be difficult etc., and seeing how they react.

You could then gently inquire as to where they would like to see themselves ending up, if a similar situation arose. Depending on how that went, you might suggest that it's probably no harm to chat in a bit more detail on what might be some of the options for themselves in the future should they become dependent.

While you might have some very clear ideas as to what needs to happen and how, remember it's not about you imposing these on your parent. Instead, it's about having a dialogue in which you both participate and trying to negotiate a solution that best meets their needs for adequate care. Paramount for them are their needs for a sense of choice and connection to the world they are familiar with.

Be willing to listen and hear them out

Focus on listening empathically rather than getting your views across in the first instance. Getting them to open up about their real concerns, anxieties and needs, is a crucial first step. It might seem easier to simply say 'Why don't you look at having someone come in and look after you' but you need them to buy in into the idea. The best way of getting that is firstly to allow them to vent their concerns, have them acknowledged by you and then demonstrate your willingness to really understand where they are coming from.

Take adequate time to hear their viewpoints and to really demonstrate listening and acknowledgement of their concerns. For example, if they say 'They mightn't look after me well', rather than dismissing this or trying to point out what you see as the reality that 'they are all professional people, they wouldn't do that' instead, just listen and empathise with this concern. Better to say something like 'So I can see a big worry for you is that they know what they are doing and they care for you properly, yes, I can see that that's something very important for you'.

Acknowledge and tease out their concerns

Don't get locked into polarized discussions where you are trying to come up with logical arguments to get them to do something. Positional statements like 'I'm not going to have a stranger in my house' are much more an expression of anxiety, concerns, fears rather than a logically worked out decision. Explore what's beneath their position using questions and reflective listening statements rather than getting into arguing back. 'What is it that would worry you about having a stranger' …'So you'd be afraid they wouldn't care enough?' …what else would concern you?

Partner with them in exploring solutions

See the discussion as one where you are jointly exploring and seeking solutions rather than one where you are in the role of persuading or trying to 'get them' to do something. Steer the discussion towards a collaborative brain storming to come up with a range of options rather than one where you are trying to get them to come to the conclusion that you've already thought up of. 'Let's think about all the possible options that you might have to support you when you are less able to move around…what ideas do you have?

Give it time. Having to come to terms with the realities of old age, ill health and mortality is a huge challenge in itself, not to mind having to adjust to lifestyle changes in line with this. Think in terms of having a number of short, supportive exchanges over a number of months or even years rather than one big meeting to get it all said and sorted.

Take ownership of your own needs and anxieties

Ultimately, it's their life and while you might have concerns and anxieties about that, you need to see these as yours and find your own way of dealing with them rather than just wanting to impose a solution on your aging parent(s) so you sleep easier at night.

Talking amongst siblings/family

Likewise it can be tempting to postpone or not bother with having any discussions with siblings around your parents future. However, having the conversation amongst the family members when there isn't the pressure of any immediate crisis or issue is much easier. It means that you can ask a lot of open and hypothetical questions that promote discussion and for which there is no need to find immediate resolution. It can also be something can happen stages rather than all at once.

It might start with just a casual question to test the waters and get a sense of where each of your siblings is in terms of openness to discussing the subject.

While it may be something you have been considering for a while and have even developed some ideas about it, it may be a new and unhappy topic to some of your siblings. They will need time to think about and come to terms in their own heads with the idea of having to have such a discussion and won't be ready to launch into a full-scale review of all the issues straight away.

Involve everyone in any discussions

Ideally it's best to involve all the family, even if the resulting decisions are that one or two members take a more active role in day-to-day care and decisions that have to be made. There should be some arrangement for all siblings to sit together and have a round table discussion about what might need to happen.

One of the key challenges of such family discussions is that the conversation can easily get sidetracked into past issues, recriminations, old hurts etc. Another dynamic that can arise is that people fall back into childhood roles e.g. the older siblings perhaps leading and taking a very active role in making decisions or a quieter more reserved person reverting to their 'silent compliant' childhood role.

If this is likely to happen then unless you are already very skilled at managing the conversation, it might be worth having an external person to support you in the conversation. As an external neutral, they can set up a framework for the discussion which ensures that everyone will have a chance to express their views and have those heard by the group in a safe, non-threatening way.

Be prepared for emotions such as resentment and guilt

While you yourself may have a caring and positive feeling towards your aging parent, there may be family members who do not feel the same as you and who may have some level of old resentment from things that happened to them for which they still might blame your parents.

On the other hand, you yourself might feel less than caring and find it hard to have to contemplate getting into this role with your parents. It's important to become really aware of your own feelings, intentions, and emotional reaction towards your parents and take responsibility for these feelings and how they have the potential to influence negatively your approach in dealing with your parents.

In raising the issue amongst siblings, one of the key emotions that often surfaces in discussions about parents is that of guilt, particularly in the case of members of your family who might have spent the last ten or twenty years living quite a distance away and not getting to spend a lot of time with their parents. If people are harbouring their own guilt about their parents, then it is very easy to trigger this off in any discussion and a likely reaction to being triggered about one's guilt is to get defensive.

Don't get trapped in defensive arguing

If you raise the issue about an aging parent and are met with a defensive response, then rather than engaging in an argument around it, simply acknowledge what they are saying, show some understanding and then clarify, that you are simply trying to have an open and honest conversation about what will happen in terms of their future care. It can be helpful to agree some simple 'ground rules' around the discussion e.g. that each person speaks respectfully and listens to the other etc.

Be prepared for emotional reactions when this topic is raised. The best way to deal with those is to try and see them for what they are, a communication from that person that they are themselves experiencing some emotion around the subject and that they are finding that difficult.

Adopt a listening, empathic approach that will allow them to vent a little around their own upset. You might say 'I can see that this topic is hard for all of us to discuss' or 'I can see you are feeling reluctant around having this discussion…that's understandable'. This kind of reflective statement will give them space and encouragement a bit more. Simply by sitting and listening to this in a non-judgmental way will help them to move beyond the emotions and get to a place where they can talk it through rationally.

Conclusion

The changing dynamic between a parent and adult child or children where the dependent(s) becomes the carer is a huge emotional challenge. However handling this sensitively in a open and transparent mannor not only leads to better solutions but can enrich the relationship between parent and adult child.

It can also help you become clear on how you would like to be cared for yourself in the future and provide a model for your children on how to handle this process in a caring and supportive way

Profile: Mary Rafferty, BEd MSocSc MMII

Mediator, Coach, Trainer, Conflict Resolution and Prevention Specialist...

For almost a decade, Mary Rafferty has worked as a mediator with organisations to enable and empower them to prevent, manage or cope with conflict and difficult relationships.

Based in Co. Leitrim, Mary's work as a business mediator takes her all over Ireland and she has worked on conflict mediation from Dublin to Sligo and many places in between. Her interventions have been in both the public sector and the private sector from businesses to multi-nationals.

Why choose Consensus Mediation?

Mary has almost thirty years of hands-on, people-focused work experience. Having trained as a teacher, she spent ten years working with both adults and children in Ireland and in Germany. She transitioned to Social Work in the nineties and worked in the conflict- and stress- ridden but rewarding area of child protection for almost another ten years.

Having taken numerous courses in the field of conflict mediation and resolution and people-relationships, Mary brings a huge amount of wisdom, intuition and knowledge to her work with clients. Furthermore, far from being an 'add-on' tool, Mary provides a dedicated service combining her experience and expertise to helping people to prevent, deal with and resolve conflict.

CHAPTER 7
Specialist Services

Elderly people do require specialist services, just as infants and small children have specialist pediatricians, elderly people should visit specialists in geriatric medicine.

As more and more people live longer geriatric medicine is ever expanding and changing and GP's just cant keep up to date with all the advances in treatments and medications available.

Thankfully Geriatrics is currently the most sought after specialty in Ireland.

Geriatric Medicine in Ireland

Geriatric medicine has developed to become the largest specialty in Internal medicine in Ireland with 54 consultants based in general hospitals around the country. These include Dublin (18), Cork (5), Galway (2), Limerick (3) and 2 each in Letterkenny, Castlebar, Waterford, Wexford, Kilkenny, Clonmel and one each in Sligo, Cavan/Monaghan, Roscommon, Dundalk, Drogheda, Navan, Naas, Mullingar, Tullamore, Nenagh, Ballinasloe, Tralee, Bantry and Mallow. The professional association representing geriatricians is the Irish Society of Physicians in Geriatric Medicine, founded in 1979.

Psychiatry of Old Age has been developing since the late 1980's, and there are now consultant Psychiatrists of Old Age in Dublin and posts in Cork, Limerick, Ennis, Cavan, Waterford, Portlaoise and Donegal.

There are full and associate chairs in geriatric medicine (Prof Rose Anne Kenny, Prof Davis Coakley, Prof Desmond O'Neill) and Psychiatry of Old Age (Prof Brian Lawlor) at the Faculty of Health Sciences, Trinity College Dublin
http://indigo.ie/~arhc/arhcger.html - top

Geriatric/gerontological training

Training for consultant physicians is in both internal medicine and geriatric medicine. In conjunction with the Royal College of Physicians in Ireland, the ISPGM has developed a Diploma in Medicine of the Elderly, a qualification designed for family doctors who would have responsibility for older people outside the general hospital, ie as the Medical Officer for an extended-care institution.

Specialist training in the care of older people is also available for nurses, with a Diploma and Masters in Gerontological Nursing from Trinity College Dublin, diplomas in Gerontological Nursing at UCC, UCD and NUIG and a Certificate in Nursing for the Elderly from St Mary's Hospital in Dublin.

So do request to see a geriatric specialist for eyesight, hearing, (E NT) digestion, elimination, heart and lungs (Cardiac, Thorasic) as well as bone specialists (orthopedician) and cancer specialists (Oncology)

Mental health is the usual focus for old age with many more people being afflicted with Dementia and Alzheimer's, however as their main organs and systems fail they do need other specialist input.

Having a cohesive team or a family GP who has some good background in Geriatric care will assist your Mum and Dad enormously as many older people are on multiple medications and some people may need to try a few combinations before getting the right combination for them.

Medication and medical needs must be assessed every 6 months for those in the late 70's to 80's as their needs can change fast.

As a child of an elderly parent I am always monitoring my mother, as she is very reluctant to visit her doctor or tell him anything she feels is not urgent or important.

Also she can very easily forget now, to report something that happened, as she forgets more easily when under stress sitting in front of him. Often he is talking about other stuff or rushing through a big patient load.

In the old days the doctor knew everyone and usually saw you in the village shop or at Mass and would be much more aware of changes taking place.

Nowadays with new medical centers you rarely see the same doctor twice in a year.

This is why we as adult children must now be educated to notice the signs, be aware of what needs to be done and be able to assist our Mum's and Dad's get the care they need.

Many Pharmacies now are improving their service and include blister packs with the various pill combinations, in doses in segments to be taken at various times thorough the day, this is great for elderly people as they get a weeks medication on one card.

Each card is marked by days and on top times of the day using symbols like suns and moons and knife and forks.

This means they can see at a glance if today is Thursday have they had their pill after lunch or before bed.

This really helps as forgetting to take the medication at the right time is reduced, as is skipping it or overdosing, if they forgot.

I have included as much information on current help available and resources for geriatric medicine, physicians, and signs and symptoms to look for at www.careformumanddad.com

CHAPTER 8
Nursing Home Versus Home Care

Your guide to getting the very best whichever you choose.

I have covered lots of information on this subject in earlier chapters when we looked at all the services available; we also have looked at the pros and cons of each.

In this chapter I would like you to have all the information you will need to decide on which is the best solution for your Mum or Dad.

I will cover what you should be looking for, in both a nursing home and a home care provider.

I have prepared lists of questions to ask and checklists of important criteria to ensure your Mum or Dad get the best care wherever they are.

I have even included information to help you, protect your Mum and Dad, by creating a proper care plan, being aware of pitfalls and all legal aspects of hiring someone, should this be something you would like to consider.

I have prepared numerous resources, checklists and questionnaires to help you, and your parents to decide which would be the best option for everyone, based on your individual circumstances.

The initial gathering of information is really important no matter what option you decide to choose as we are all individuals and we need to keep our autonomy for as long as possible and being in a situation where the person or centre delivering care, has in depth knowledge of the clients individual likes and needs make the caring situation much more successful.

I have a client who is an elderly gentleman with Dementia, he is incontinent and loves to chat, he lives on top of a mountain and has always had horses and sheep. The family put him into a nursing home for a short respite and he called his daughter daily crying "Take me home I will die in here" the family opted for a couple of days a week to assist the family who were his main caregivers.

He is happy and thriving, as someone like him will feel alone and alienated when cooped up in a home when he is used to open fields and animals.

Nursing Home

The first consideration once you have decided this is the best option for you is location.

You will need to consider where is best for all the family to visit, travelling times, traffic congestion, ease of access and if family are coming in from overseas will it be easy for them to visit too.

If you need to use public transport is it close to trains or bus routes?

Being close to their home is not really important, it is much more important that your parents can have regular visits with all the family.

- ✓ The next thing to consider is how visitor friendly is the nursing home?
- ✓ Would you be able to bring children?
- ✓ Are there strict visitor rules and times or is the home very flexible regarding family visits?
- ✓ Are there spaces inside and outside for having a visit or will you be confined to their room?
- ✓ Will they be sharing a room?
- ✓ Can they have their own TV?
- ✓ Can they bring special items to create their own personal space?
- ✓ How "Homely" is this place or is it more like a private hospital?
- ✓ Can your Mum and dad get a cup of tea or be assisted in making some hot drinks any time of the day?
- ✓ Is their dining area like a nice restaurant or more like a school canteen?
- ✓ Are there outdoor areas to sit and walk?
- ✓ Can your Mum and dad grow any plants if they like this?
- ✓ Could they bring a pet?
- ✓ Or are there communal pets like dogs and cats, does the home face an open field where they can observe animals.
- ✓ What about the resident's do they look happy?
- ✓ Are they clean?
- ✓ Does there seem to be a bit of a buzz with activities or interactions?
- ✓ Is there a smell of urine?
- ✓ Are residents squabbling or some being aggressive?
- ✓ Do they all look drugged and dopey?
- ✓ How about the staff are they gentle and kind?
- ✓ Did you witness interactions between staff and clients?

✓ Is there a sense of "HOME" a sense of belonging and laughter?

✓ If you are sensitive can you feel a happy vibe?

✓ Are the rooms like home, is there wallpaper or pictures on the walls?

✓ Are the chairs in small family like groupings or a big room with chairs all lined up or in a circle?

✓ How about outings, activities and socializing?

✓ What extra costs are involved for additional, services, craft /hobby materials, laundry or outings that not included in the weekly charges.

✓ How much will these add to the weekly costs.

✓ What if your Mum or Dad has to be hospitalized suddenly for a few weeks?

✓ Do you still have to pay?

✓ If so how much?

✓ If they wish to leave what is the notice period?

✓ Are they approved so you can apply for funding or grants, (such as The Fair Deal Scheme)

✓ Have they been rated upon inspection by HIQUA?

✓ Are there waiting lists or available beds?

✓ Have you looked at their contracts?

✓ How will you, and your family fund this?

✓ How long will you and the family be able to fund this care?

✓ Really, the question to ask yourselves is would we be happy here?

Home Care

If this is the option for you there are also things you must consider like….

➢ Costs of maintaining their home, plus paying for care?

➢ Will this be viable and if so for how long?

➢ Can your parents release equity from their home, to cover care costs?

- ➢ Can you obtain funding from the HSE with a HOME CARE PACKAGE?
- ➢ Do you have adequate space so a carer can have their own room?
- ➢ How do your parents feel about someone living with them?
- ➢ What are their fears?
- ➢ What are your fears?
- ➢ How did you find the company?
- ➢ How do they recruit their staff, do they perform security (GARDA) checking, reference checking, what kind of training and qualifications do they require their staff to have?
- ➢ Do they train their staff themselves?
- ➢ If they train staff themselves are these carers experienced in one to one care and if so how many years experience have they?
- ➢ Are you given a couple of carers to choose from?
- ➢ Is there any trial period?
- ➢ Are you willing to answer detailed questions in order to assist the company to get the right match of carer, and get off to a flying start as teething troubles are mostly eliminated when good preparations are in place.
- ➢ Have they a clear terms of Business document you can view before signing anything?
- ➢ What are their terms if your Mum or Dad has to be hospitalized suddenly?
- ➢ Are there surcharges for public holidays?
- ➢ How do you feel about the service provider from your first contact?
- ➢ Have you been given, a clear outline of what to expect, have all the charges and contracts been available for inspection before making a decision?
- ➢ If the situation is not an emergency was a home visit conducted to assess your parents care needs and situation?

> Do they employ their staff and pay all the contributions for their employees, and pay holiday pay and cover their staff with a good comprehensive specialized carer insurance? (This means the carer is insured when she/he is working in your home)

> How is their staff and client retention?

> What monitoring and reporting systems do they have in place?

> Do they have clear, written and downloadable or available materials on Health and Safety, Customer Care Charter, Carers Handbook, Lone workers Policies, Complaints Policy on their website that you can view or download?

> Do you feel confident and comfortable dealing with this company, and feel there are good measures in place for you and your parents protection, based on what clients have said and your initial dealings with them.

Hiring Privately

Hiring privately is the most stressful as you need to be really clear on what your requirements are, you also need to be able to do background checks and be able to verify their training and experience.

1. How will you monitor the carer?
2. How many hours will he/ she work is this legal.
3. How can you protect yourself from an unscrupulous employee who want to exploit you or your parents and may even take you to the Labour Court for working more hours than they were paid for. (Their word against yours and the employer is often seen as a slave driver wanting to hire on the cheap and exploit the worker especially if she or he is a foreigner)
4. Setting yourself up legally as an employer, paying contributions and making payments from deductions to

the Revenue, carrying insurance and paying for sick leave and holiday pay.

5. Setting up a care plan and setting boundaries and having a professional work arrangement is not easy without a clear structure and understanding of working hours, duties, and risks.

Alternatively you can approach a specialized recruitment company who will do all of this difficult part for you and set up contracts and can give you advice as an employer.

Home Help Recruitment is the recruitment arm of Affordable Bespoke Care Solutions Limited and we go through the same stringent process of recruitment as when we will employ the carers ourselves.

Usually you will pay a one off fee or a percentage of the annual salary, or some other form of agreed payment for providing services.

You will then pay your staff yourself and this means you are paying only wages plus employer contributions and not agency rates.

This could mean a saving of €2 per hour up to €8 per hour depending on what the care company charges. Therefore based on 10 hours per day you could save between €300–€560 per week which can be up to €29,000 in a year.

So even paying a couple of thousand in initial fees can represent a substantial saving.

Some of the disadvantages can be:-

If your carer gets sick or decides to leave suddenly a few months after she/he starts you have lost your investment and most companies will only cover a 90 day guarantee.

The carer starts to get lazy or insolent, as there were no proper rules laid down.

The carer takes extended leave of 4-6 weeks; you will need a short-term solution, which will result in additional costs.

You get a home care package (the HSE will only pay to an approved agency not directly to a carer or the family)
★ *see complimentary booklet at* <u>*www.care-for-mum-and-dad.com*</u> *for international information on grants*

With a service arrangement or a nursing home you know your parents are guaranteed the level of service you agreed upon, no mater what happens, as replacement staff of a similar nature will be supplied by the company, which means your parents have a seamless care service and you have complete peace of mind.

Home Help Recruitment is a specialized agency supplying care staff nationally, and have taken into consideration all the possible disadvantages and have put together unique and customized plans to assist you to hire someone yourself and reduce or cut out the headaches of being an employer, and of staff taking holidays or getting sick.
Visit www.homehelprecruitment.com

Summary

Re Read the Chapter "Einy, Meany,Miny, Mo" which covers topics to help the family explore and discuss what your parents care needs may be, then check out the resources on the website www.care-for-mum-and-dad.com

Working through the materials and having the discussions will help you to come to the best possible solution where your Mum and Dad will be happiest and you will have peace of mind knowing you have done your very best for them.

Care is a very personal choice and people do need different levels of care as they get older or less mobile among other things.

The important thing is to gain agreement and clarity on what your parents really want, and is it possible?

Do you have guidelines for when its time to change or upgrade care arrangements?

Have you discussed when in future certain situations arise whereby care or space parameters have been reached with regards to, dementia, incontinence, mobility problems and current space and facilities to manage their care needs, what is the next step?

Finances and funding, how long can your parent's resources last to maintain their care?

What options are available?

Government Funding?

Release of equity from the family home?

Insurance?

Family contributions?

By now we have covered most aspects of care, renovations, legal and financial and getting to grips with family communication so if you do the groundwork, and have clear plans this will result in less stress for the whole family.

Check out our websites to give you ideas, on what's available plus costs involved.

www.casacarers.ie

www.homehelprecruitment.com

www.affordablehomecare.com

My Last chapter is about the end and saying goodbye and preparing for the inevitable

CHAPTER 9
Saying Goodbye

What is hospice and palliative care?

Although death is a natural part of life, the thought of dying understandably still frightens many people, and their families. Often older people's greatest fears are to imagine being in pain and feeling lonely spending their final days in the cold, sterile environment of a hospital far from family, friends and all that they know and love.

There are however, some older people who are unwilling to be in hospital to undergo more tests and treatments that are not producing any answers or improvements. In these cases they may feel they would rather be home in comfort with palliative care to keep them comfortable and pain free.

Some hospitals, nursing homes, and other health care facilities do provide hospice care onsite; in most cases hospice or Palliative care is provided in the patient's own home. This enables your Mum or Dad to spend their final days in a familiar, comfortable environment, surrounded by their loved ones who can focus more fully on them with the support of hospice or specially trained care staff.

Hospice care represents a compassionate approach to end–of–life care, enhancing the quality of remaining life and enabling your Mum or Dad to live as fully and as comfortably as possible.

Seeking hospice and palliative care isn't about giving up hope or hastening death, but rather a way to get the most appropriate care in the last phase of life.

Hospice is traditionally an option for people whose life expectancy is six months or less, mostly associated with cancer and involves palliative care (pain and symptom relief) rather than ongoing curative measures, enabling your Mum or Dad to live their last days to the fullest, with purpose, dignity, grace, and support.

Talking about hospice and palliative care

For many families, death remains a taboo subject, and even though they are aware their Mum or Dad is dying they refuse to talk about it or start any planning, if and when he or she passes. Consequently, for many older people, who may develop a terminal illness or are admitted after a fall and contract a bad infection (MRSA's or super bugs) end up spending prolonged periods in hospital and even dying there when they would have much preferred to be at home, the norm unfortunately is still to die in hospital, where they continue to receive treatment that is either unwanted or ineffective.

Beautiful young people are accidents of nature, But beautiful old people are works of art.
— Eleanor Roosevelt Quotes

My personal experience with my mother was that the hospital could not diagnose what or where her source of infection was coming from, yet were unwilling to let her go home, as they wanted to conduct as many tests as required as to give them then answers they were looking for.

I met other people who had had similar experiences and had to fight to bring their loved one home.

Once home and under their GP many people recover much quicker.

If they are not going to recover then I am sure they would rather end their days in their own bed surrounded by those who love them.

Many families still remain reluctant to even discuss the possibility of hospice care or palliative care. By doing so means you are considering the possibility of losing them and no one want to be the first to state the obvious, as many families feel that by talking about death, means you are inviting it or expecting it and siblings can turn against one another, with accusations of not caring, hence no one talks, no one plans.

However, it is a fact most people would prefer to die in their own homes, surrounded by loved ones.

Some families who do choose hospice care often do so only for the last few days of life, and later regret not having more time saying goodbye to their loved one.

This is why I have emphasized all through this book the urgency and importance of being prepared with information and having discussed all situations and possibilities. When the whole family are clear about your loved ones preferences for treatment or end of life care. You will all be free to devote your energy to care, compassion and saying goodbye.

In Ireland the HSE provide Palliative Care and Hospice services www.hse.ie

Legal and Financial

I have previously mentioned my father died without a will and this will leave the family in a complicated mess.By having the legal and financial affairs of your Mum or Dad in order will mean less aggravation and stress when you are already trying to cope with loss and bereavement.

I have invited specialists to cover all aspect of preparing for these matters and some excellent tools to assist you.
To obtain these visit www.care-for-mum-and-dad.com

I would highly recommend a living will especially to cover the last days and if your parent's short term memories are beginning to deteriorate, then they will still be able to have their wishes complied with, even after they have slipped into their own little worlds.

Things you should consider are invasive treatments that may cause more distress then short term or minimal benefits derived, do they

97

want to be resuscitated? It may seem morbid but this way you and your loved ones do get to have a say, them do get to have a say, and are not at the mercy of hospital policies or other peoples decisions.

Planning the Funeral

Planning a funeral is more complicated than you may think. Even when death is expected, it nevertheless always seems to be unreal. The fact that it has actually happened, your loved one has finally gone, you will be experiencing so many emotions, and not everyone grieves the same way.

My sister and I laughed at everything and all day, it was a kind of hysterical reaction, I being the eldest wanted to keep things light for my Mum so humour and laughter was my way of getting through the death and funeral. It really hit me hard after it was all over then the fact that my darling daddy was gone, we couldn't share any more experiences with him and it all happened so fast.

Grieving family members and friends may be confronted with dozens of funeral planning decisions – all of which must be made quickly, and typically under great emotional duress.

What kind of funeral should it be?

What funeral provider should you use?

Should you bury or cremate the body?

What other arrangements should you plan?

Whom should you notify?

And, as unpleasant as it may sound, how much is it all going to cost and where will the money come from to pay for it?

Knowing and following your Mum or Dads wishes can alleviate some of this decision-making stress.

Following the funeral, your Mum and Dad's financial affairs will need to be finalized, and the information that you may have gathered at "The Meeting" will be invaluable in completing this task.

There are lots of things you will need when a person passes.

To help you I have prepared a checklist, which encompasses everything you will need to do.

Ideally, this should be discussed with your Mum and Dad when you are doing your planning at "The Meeting".

Trust me, this discussion or many discussions you will need to have to sort out all of your parent's affairs will be the best thing you ever did.

Then when one or the other or both pass the preparation you invested in will be invaluable.

If you have followed all the instructions in this book then all misunderstandings, old hurts, and grievances should have been healed by now and resolved.

So that now the family can focus on saying goodbye, and celebrating the cherished memories and the life of your loved one.

This is the time as a family, to be remembering all the good times, the struggles you all survived. To remember the love shared, the special occasions, like weddings, christenings, Christmases, holidays and so forth.

Some times its silly little things you remember very often from childhood, remembering is good.

If you find bad memories surfacing, its time to forgive and let go as your parents are only human and were doing the best they could at the time or perhaps they were not loving warm kind parents, however they were still human and as such filled with weaknesses and imperfection.

Only in forgiveness and accepting their imperfections and learning to grow from their mistakes can we make things better for our own children.

Forgiveness releases you from anger, hurt, disappointment and regrets.

In many families death causes not only the grief of loss but sibling rivalry and greed surface making it the most stressful and horrible occasion.

Anger, frustration and egos clash and this will cause huge distress if you have a surviving parent.

My personal views on death.

I believe the soul is eternal that our souls are the perfect part that is created and connected to God or Source energy.

Therefore I believe in Life After Death and also in past lives,

I believe we live many physical lives to learn, we often travel in soul groups and choose to reincarnate with the same souls in many lives to learn and grow.

I believe my first husband and I had many lives together not always as husband and wife but as family, our soul contract this life was to have our 3 children.

I have studied and worked using therapy with past lives and we can make sense of things today when we get glimpses of information from the past.

Is all of this true?? Who knows for sure?

However, if it helps to improve our understandings and we grow in a positive way then to me what is important is the results.

My beliefs and discussions about past lives and life after death are not within the scope of this book, yet as you may have noticed,

I like to share my own personal experiences and have opened up myself to you, as I want you to know, my intention is to help families be prepared with information to assist in choosing the right care.

I also would love if this book helped families to heal their differences, make peace and let their aged parents enjoy the love and bonds that may have been fractured in the past.

If all families used the information in this book and the extra FREE Bonuses, then more families would be having these discussions sooner rather than later.

Families would be able to have their estate planning, care choices, living wills and funerals all prepared for in advance of any critical situation.

This means there would be no shocks or recriminations after they pass.

Then the funeral can be the time to say goodbye, to bond closer as a family and to celebrate the life of your loved one.

Another great activity to do with elderly parents is record their stories, have them transcribed and add photos to compile lovely family heirlooms for future generations.

Based on my beliefs, the soul being eternal helps me, as I believe my loved one is still with me.

I believe the physical body dies and decays but their spirit lives on and they are still with us when we need them or at family events.

My mother says I creep her out, but I talk to my Dad often and at Christmas I may raise a toast to include and remember close family that have passed.

My clients with Alzheimer's, love when I visit them, they may have no clue who I am, but I feel I connect with their soul energy.

I don't see the disease I see the person and it's a very feeling type of energy exchange.

Post Funeral Duties

After the funeral there are still many tasks to be completed, like cancelling policies, bank accounts, pensions or benefit payments, grants, car insurance the list is very long, however I have prepared a comprehensive check list and information sheet so you should, by this stage be very well organized and most of the information is to hand and the task of performing these last tasks for your deceased loved one will be less stressful and arduous.

Grieving And Bereavement

Grief is the normal internal feeling one may experience in reaction to a loss, while bereavement is the state of having experienced that loss.

Losing someone you love or care deeply about is very painful. You may experience all kinds of difficult emotions and it may feel like the pain and sadness you're experiencing will never let up.

I remember about a year after my father had passed I was in a supermarket with my Mum and she just welled up, fighting back tears she told me she just had an overwhelming feeling about my dad.

She told me on and off this happens she may hear a song or see a movie they had enjoyed together, triggers of memories of a shared life.

You may wonder what happened in the supermarket? I lived in Ireland and they had, had many happy summers together in Ireland visiting my grandmother in Leitrim.

These are normal reactions to a significant loss. But while there is no right or wrong way to grieve, there are healthy ways to cope with the pain that, in time, can renew you and permit you to move on.

In 1969, psychiatrist Elisabeth Kübler-Ross introduced what became known as the "five stages of grief." These stages of grief were based on her studies of the feelings of patients facing terminal illness, but many people have generalized them to other types of negative life changes and losses, such as the death of a loved one or a break-up.

The five stages of grief:

Denial: "This can't be happening to me."
Anger: "Why is this happening? Who is to blame?"
Bargaining: "Make this not happen, and in return I will ____."
Depression: "I'm too sad to do anything."
Acceptance: "I'm at peace with what happened."

If you are experiencing any of these emotions following a loss, it may help to know that your reaction is natural and that you'll heal in time. However, not everyone who is grieving goes through all of these stages – and that's okay. Contrary to popular belief, you do not have to go through each stage in order to heal. In fact, some people resolve their grief without going through any of these stages. And if you do go through these stages of grief, you probably won't experience them in a neat, sequential order, so don't worry about what you "should" be feeling or which stage you're supposed to be in.

Kübler-Ross herself never intended for these stages to be a rigid framework that applies to everyone who mourns. In her last book before her death in 2004, she said of the five stages of grief, "*They were never meant to help tuck messy emotions into neat packages. They are responses to loss that many people have, but there is not a typical response to loss, as there is no typical loss. Our grieving is as individual as our lives.*"

Common symptoms of grief

While loss affects people in different ways, many people experience the following symptoms when they're grieving. Just remember that almost anything that you experience in the early stages of grief is normal – including feeling like you're going crazy, feeling like you're in a bad dream, or questioning your religious beliefs.

Shock and disbelief – Right after a loss, it can be hard to accept what happened. You may feel numb, have trouble believing that the loss really happened, or even deny the truth. If someone you love has died, you may keep expecting them to show up, even though you know they're gone.

Sadness – Profound sadness is probably the most universally experienced symptom of grief. You may have feelings of emptiness, despair, yearning, or deep loneliness. You may also cry a lot or feel emotionally unstable.

Guilt – You may regret or feel guilty about things you did or didn't say or do. You may also feel guilty about certain feelings (e.g. feeling relieved when the person died after a long, difficult illness). After a death, you may even feel guilty for not doing something to prevent the death, even if there was nothing more you could have done.

Anger – Even if the loss was nobody's fault, you may feel angry and resentful. If you lost a loved one, you may be angry at yourself, God, the doctors, or even the person who died for abandoning you. You may feel the need to blame someone for the injustice that was done to you.

Fear – A significant loss can trigger a host of worries and fears. You may feel anxious, helpless, or insecure. You may even have panic attacks. The death of a loved one can trigger fears about your own mortality, of facing life without that person, or the responsibilities you now face alone.

Physical symptoms – We often think of grief as a strictly emotional process, but grief often involves physical problems, including fatigue, nausea, lowered immunity, weight loss or weight gain, aches and pains, and insomnia.

Ways Of Coping

There is no one way for all, and definitely time does heal.

Like depression you need to take an active part in helping yourself get through the pain of loss and all the other symptoms that you may or may not experience.

Making sure you eat, regularly and not just quick convenience meals. Otherwise your health will suffer and you will just be in this horrible place for longer than you should.

Plan for triggers like anniversaries, if you are religious use rituals and ways that help you during these days.

My way was to have lots of internal dialog with my Dad, by asking his advice, telling him my hopes and dreams, and asking for his help.

I talk to my Guardian Angel too and other Angels and God, this is my way.

My mother prays Rosaries and Novenas.

Cultural and religious practices do help us when we are grieving or going through difficult times.

get help - there are many groups and counselors who will help you get through this.

Turn to your family and close friends.

Everything is Ok crying, screaming, and feeling angry, frustrated or afraid.

Let it run its own course, you will have good days and bad and laughter is always a great medicine.

Watch comedies, read joke books. You are alive and that's great too, don't feel guilty if you're having fun

Final Thoughts

I love watching shows like "Crossing Over" where mediums pass messages to the loved ones still alive from the "other side" and these are always messages of love, encouragement and acknowledgment of love.

For me this helped me so much, knowing my Dad was there.

Incidentally he believed in Death no afterlife, we discussed this and he was adamant when the lights went out you were gone.

On his deathbed, I reminded him. "Dad if there is life after death let me know, give me a sign I said "Knock 3 Times"

After he passed my sister and I were coming from the hospital driving on the motorway, her car alarm went off, her doors all locked and this happened 3 times in succession.

This happened only that one time.
Was this his way to let me know, there is an afterlife, after all?

Never.
We never lose our loved ones.
They accompany us; they don't disappear from our lives.
We are merely in different rooms.

Paul Coelho

Extra Bonus Comprehensive Funeral Planning worksheet available at www.care-for-mum-and-dad.com

Afterword

I know that if you bought and read this book you are a really caring person and clearly want the best for your Mum or Dad.

I truly hope this little book and all the FREE bonus materials will help you to be prepared and help alleviate stress for the whole family, now or when the time comes.

Thank you for letting me share my knowledge and experiences with you and and if I am I would be happy to answer questions you may still have.

You can contact me visa www.care-for-mum-and-dad-.com

You can also leave feedback and comments here too.